THE HAND OF THE LORD

CHRISTUS

This statue of Jesus Christ stands in the rotunda of the North Visitors' Center on Temple Square in Salt Lake City, Utah. Commissioned by The Church of Jesus Christ of Latter-day Saints, it is a marble replica of Christus Consolator, *which was carved by Bertel Thorvaldsen in 1821. The original statue is located in the Church of Our Lady in Copenhagen, Denmark.*

The Hand of the Lord

Testimonies of His Blessings in Our Lives

by the Women of the
Apple Valley Ward
of
The Church of Jesus Christ
of Latter-day Saints

Apple Valley, Minnesota
2013

Edited by Ginger Hamer
Cover design by John C. Hamer
Cover photos by Logan Walker, loganwalkerphoto.com

© 2013 Apple Valley Ward Relief Society, Lakeville Minnesota Stake
    of The Church of Jesus Christ of Latter-day Saints

This work is not an official publication of The Church of Jesus Christ of Latter-day
Saints. The views expressed herein are the responsibility of the authors and do not
necessarily represent the position of the Church.

ISBN-13: 978-1482776959
ISBN-10: 1482776952

*"Yet will I not forget thee.
Behold, I have graven thee
upon the palms of my hands."*

Isaiah 49:15-16

TABLE OF CONTENTS

FINDING OUR WAY

The Beginning of a New Life, *Lisa Young*	7
His Promises Are Sure, *Lucy Ekanem*	11
The Unlikely Convert, *Nancy Gayder*	14
A Constant Guide, *Tonia Gintz*	17
What I've Learned Along the Way, *Dianne Anderson*	24
Unshackled, *Caitlin Robinson*	29
Changing Points in My Life, *Frances Davis*	32
My Story, *Diane Johnson*	37
My Search Began in Sixth Grade, *Jacquelyn A. Kellington*	41
Our Daughter Led the Way, *Norma Storland*	47

RECEIVING ANSWERS TO PRAYER

The Cell Phone, *Jacquelyn A. Kellington*	51
The Joy My Children Give Me, *Abby Villanueva*	55
Prayer, *Heather Graham*	59
He Hears My Prayers, *Megan Stotts*	63
The Holy Ghost, *Ainsley Davis*	66
The Lost Folder, *Holly Thatcher*	67
Alice, the Snake, *Emily Tennant*	74
The Power of Prayer, *Lucy Ekanem*	79
Blessed with a Needed Gift, *Ginger Hamer*	82
A Child's Prayer, *Jacquelyn A. Kellington*	85
He Continues to Walk by My Side, *Cathy Tennant*	87
The Magically, Perfectly Clean House, *Loni Davis*	90

THE HAND OF THE LORD

BEING GUIDED ON LIFE'S PATH

The Road Back, *Lynnette Howze*	95
The Right Place at the Right Time, *Mindy Barringer*	99
The Lord's Plan for Me, *DeAnna Larson*	101
From Rebellion to Understanding, *Ginger Hamer*	107
Heavenly Father Found Me, *Polly J. Parsons*	112
Where He Needs Us to Be, *Nikhom Bailey*	115
Growing in the Spirit, *Tamara Clifford*	117
The Incredible Job, *Erika Hogge*	121

SHOWING FAITH THROUGH OBEDIENCE

A Tithing Miracle, *Sonia Glaser*	127
Tender Mercies Follow Faith, *Amy Meyer*	130
The Hot Tub Modesty Test, *Anna Pugmire*	133
A Lesson on Service, *Becky White*	135
The Lord Blesses Those Who Strive to Serve Him	137
Ashley Flake	

LISTENING TO THE SPIRIT

Water in the Desert, *Kourtney Graham*	141
Blessed for Following a Prompting, *Caroline Korth*	145
A Prompting in the Night, *Jacqueline A. Kellington*	148
Learn, Listen, Walk, *Merle Pratt*	152

KNOWING THE TENDER MERCIES OF GOD

He Knew, *Cindy Singer*	159
The Lord Is There for Me, *Maria Gandarilla*	161

Table of Contents

Sad to Glad, *Allie Pugmire*	163
Trust in the Lord, *Jessica Peterson*	165
Temple Flower Gardens, *Cara Gordhamer*	168
Only with the Help of the Lord, *Sabrina Herrmann*	169
The Lord Is Watching over Me, *Vicki McGregor*	171
My Miracle Husband, *Nancy Gayder*	174
Our Miracle Baby, *Krissy Schweigert*	177
Frankie, *Dannica Dufur*	181
He Sends Angels to Lift Us Up, *Josalyn McAllister*	184
God Sent People to Help Me, *Haymanot Balcha*	187
Thoughts from the Kitchen, *Marlene Gordhamer*	189
The Lord Healed My Heart, *Jacquelyn A. Kellington*	192
The Right Word at the Right Time, *EmRee Pugmire*	196

DRAWING CLOSER
TO OUR LOVING FATHER

God's Children, *Helen Manar*	201
"As a hen gathereth her chickens...," *Cher Jensen*	203
A Daughter of My Heavenly Father *Shekinah Villanueva*	205
His Enveloping Love, *Noël Hosman*	207
Sunset Messages, *Jessica Friedman*	209
A Daughter of God, *Marissa Stotts*	211
My Testimony Rests on God's Love, *Heather Leavitt*	213
Moments of Stillness, *Melissa Jeanne Nielsen*	215

GAINING STRENGTH
FROM PEOPLE WE LOVE

An Example of Strength and Courage *Brooklyn Gardner*	221
My Last Trip with Mom, *Kristine Miller*	223

THE HAND OF THE LORD

Alice, *Lisa Young*	227
Remaining Faithful, *Trina Maller*	231
My Grandfather's Love, *Melissa Jeanne Nielsen*	233
Max, *Maria Stotts*	239
Grandma and Grandpa, *Loni Davis*	241
Norma Storland, 1922-2012, *Barbara Calistro*	246
My Story Begins with My Grandmother	249
Chay Douangphouxay	
Hannah Hoffman, 1919-2012, *Jacquelyn A. Kellington*	255

TEACHING OUR CHILDREN TO LOVE THE LORD

A Letter to My Sisters, *Ande Amott*	263
Everything You Need to Know, You Learn Ice Skating	268
Megan Gunyan	
My McDonald's Speech, *Frances Davis*	273
A Quiver Full, *DeAnna Larson*	275
Leaning on My Heavenly Father, *Daria Gordhamer*	280
The Eternal Nature of Peanut Butter, *Shantel Gardner*	283

TESTIFYING OF GOSPEL TRUTHS

My Baptism Day, *Emma Thatcher*	291
Come unto the Knowledge of the Truth	294
Sandra Marie Cluff	
Learning About the Savior, *Sarah Peterson*	300
We Are His Daughters, *Jannica Villanueva*	302
"O Death, Where Is Thy Sting?" *Krystal Flohr*	304
These Things I Know, *Lisa Flake*	308

Preface

This book began the day Jackie Kellington ran across her copy of *The Gift of Love,* a small book compiled by the Minneapolis Stake Relief Society in 1982. Inspired anew by the stories, she showed the book to the Relief Society presidency. They in turn presented the idea to the women of the Apple Valley Ward who responded with enthusiasm, and the project quickly expanded to include the Young Women.

Good things started to happen as soon as we began searching our memories to select a story to write. Pondering the hand of the Lord in our lives brought us closer to Him. One sister said, "It gave me cause to remember, which has strengthened my testimony and helped my heart be grateful." Another said, "Writing out my story was a blessing in disguise for me. It helped me to be more grateful for all the many blessings in my life. I needed this more than anything right now."

Our hearts were indeed grateful for the way the Holy Ghost helped us remember the many times when the Lord has intervened in our lives. Many sisters expressed the happy frustration of finding it hard to choose just one story from the countless possibilities. Several couldn't help but submit more than one.

Then, as stories began to come in, an unexpected witness emerged. We knew, of course, that the stories would be different, but they turned out to be strikingly unique to the individuals who wrote them, and the difference was much deeper than writing styles and personalities. We could clearly see that the Lord has given each of His daughters the specific experiences, answers, trials, and blessings she personally needs to bring her back to His presence. He deals with us one on one because He knows us personally. Although the stories are strikingly individual, it turns out, we can all draw meaning from each other's experiences and we are all strengthened by each other's testimonies. Like scripture stories of old that tell of God's dealings with individuals, these stories have universal appeal.

First, a word about the women themselves. We are members of The Church of Jesus Christ of Latter-day Saints. We belong to the women's organizations of the Church: the Young Women for girls ages 12 to 17 and the Relief Society for women ages 18 and older. The Apple Valley Ward is the congregation for LDS women and families who live in Apple Valley and Rosemount, Minnesota. We come from twenty-one states (with Minnesota edging out Utah thirteen to twelve) and seven countries. With this broad diversity of ages (12 to 75), backgrounds, and race, we are a good representation of the women of the Church, as well as the women of the United States.

Second, the stories, eighty-four in all, were written by seventy-one sisters of our congregation (or about eighty-five percent of those who regularly attend services and hold callings). Partici-

Preface 3

pation was entirely optional and the instructions were minimal: "Tell about a time when you saw the hand of the Lord in your life." Each sister selected her own topic with few conversations or little knowledge of what the other sisters had decided to write about. Each followed the inspiration of the Spirit in making her selection. No writing classes were held. It should be pointed out that the entire project, conceived in mid-January, was completed and sent to the publisher only four and a half months later. It is an example of how much busy Mormon women can accomplish; it is also a testament to the Church that encourages women to be educated and articulate and to value their own feelings and express them well.

Next, the organization of the book. Grouping the stories into broad themes was a challenge because most spiritual experiences —especially those described here—encompass many aspects of a person's religious life. In a single situation we might seek God's help, listen to promptings of the Spirit, exercise faith, consider good examples of people we love, and recognize divine blessings. Thus, several of the stories could fit well in several categories. We leave it to the readers to enjoy the stories for what they say, not for where they are placed.

Enjoy also the biographical information on each author. The biographies give tiny hints of our personalities and additional insights into our lives. (We have also included each author's place of birth and the names of her parents so future generations of family history researchers can identify us more easily.)

We express our appreciation to Jackie Kellington for instigating the project and for encouraging others to write; to Bishop David A. Ruff for his immediate support of the idea; to Nancy

Gayder, who before her passing helped collect stories; to Holly Thatcher for her editing skills; to Lisa Young, Heather Graham, and Melissa Nielsen of the Relief Society presidency for their initial enthusiasm for the project and for their help in tracking the stories through the submission process; and to all the sisters who had enough faith to sit down, search their experiences, and write these intimate, sacred stories. We also recognize the sisters in our ward who did not submit a story for whatever reason. They too have wonderful, compelling experiences, and we hope their stories will be told elsewhere. We are all sisters in Christ, members of a loving sisterhood, and we gain wisdom from one another.

Finally, we know that each of us could write hundreds more stories acknowledging the hand of the Lord in our lives every day. We humbly present these few in recognition of our blessings and as our witness that God lives and Jesus is the Christ. We testify that it is only in and through the Atonement of Christ that we find forgiveness for our sins and will be able to live with Him someday. For His grace we are eternally grateful.

Then I told them of the hand of my God which was good upon me...
Nehemiah 2:18

Finding Our Way

The Beginning of a New Life

BY LISA JANE YOUNG

My journal entry dated October 8, 2006

MY QUEST FOR RELIGION, something to belong to and be part of has finally come to an end. After three years of searching for answers and praying, God has directed me to The Church of Jesus Christ of Latter-day Saints.

"My first born child, Louis, was born on May 25, 2003, and unbeknown to me, at the time, I suffered with postpartum depression but convinced myself I was less of a person because I was supposedly a strong individual, hence I never dealt with it that well. Eventually my hormones died down and the depression somewhat departed. While this was happening, I realized my life needed something more. I was missing the religious piece of the puzzle and support of a church family. Living in a new country away from friends and family was very difficult and lonely.

"I set to speaking with people as often as I could about what their beliefs were. Each person I spoke with was more than happy to escort me to their church and teach me their doctrines. It was extremely confusing to me.

"One day I spoke with a friend of mine named Jackie Kellington, who I had known for some time, about finding a church. Wow, I thought, you don't have to say too much to a Mormon about looking for a church! She was so excited to invite me. It took a while but we eventually took her up on the offer.

"On the first visit I felt an overwhelming sense of peace, and a feeling of belonging. To be honest, I think I knew at this point that I wanted to be part of this loving and caring community. So what was stopping me? Simple. Outside views and my lack of knowledge to prove these opinions wrong. And so the quest continued on and off for the next two years.

"There was a day that I was sat on my balcony confused, distressed, and very upset. I spoke with God and asked Him to direct my family and me in our choices, and I prayed with fullness of my heart. At this point, praying was not something that came naturally to me; it was not something I grew up doing, unless I was in dire straits. Within moments of my prayer, who knocked at my door but the missionaries? Being skeptical, I thought this is just fate. It can't really be the work of God, can it?

"My heart softened for a moment, and I decided I would listen to what they had to share. Life became busy again and meeting with them never became a priority; there was always something else in my life more important than taking time to listen to what they had to say.

"Months passed and a new set of missionaries called by the house. Deep inside I thought, 'Lisa, this is where you are being directed,' but I still continued to fight the idea of being a Mormon. One of the missionaries left me with some scriptures to read from the Book of Mormon on faith; I had a tough time understanding it. At the time in the Minnesota Mission the missionaries were asked to read the Book of Mormon in six weeks, and I quietly took up the same challenge, but there was so much to speak about and I was so excited. I told them what I was doing!

"There were times when I would get my two children to bed and read for hours, soaking in the words of knowledge and wisdom, my heart softening with each page I read.

"September 10 I decided I wanted to quit smoking; I had been a smoker for seventeen years and had failed [to quit] many times in the past. I phoned the missionaries on Sunday evening, and quick as a tornado they came over the very next day and explained the plan to me and took my cigarettes which I was completely devastated about. They had my 3-year-old, with the help of his Little Tikes car, run over all of my cigarettes. 'Oh no,' I thought, 'what am I doing?' I felt like I was going to pass out from the panic in my chest. My son thought it was the most hysterical thing he had ever done in his short life.

"Over the next few days the missionaries were my angels on earth. They listened to my complaints and anxieties, sometimes three or four times a day, and together with God's help, I quit smoking and that was twenty-six days ago.

"The same day I gave them my cigarettes, I gave them all of my tea which was *very* difficult for a tea-drinking and crumpet-eating British woman. I also gave up coffee and alcohol at the same time!

"In the past three months I have grown so much. With all my heart and love I possess, I challenge you individually to be true to yourself and share the happiness I know you will experience by sharing the gospel with people like me. And please be patient; this is a life altering commitment we are making."

This journal entry was written one month before my husband and I were baptized and that was over six years ago now. Since then we have been sealed in the temple, which we celebrated a year after our baptism. We have also been blessed with two more children. I have personally been blessed with a mind that hungers for knowledge, and I continue to study the gospel and all it entails.

I love the gospel of Jesus Christ, and I will do whatever it takes to reach out to those who may be on a journey similar to mine who are in need of light, truth, and spiritual awareness.

Lisa Jane Young was born in Manchester, England, the daughter of Michael Joseph and Carol Belhomme. She moved to the United States in 2001 and became an American citizen in 2012. She is trained in the culinary arts, graduating six days before her first child was born. She and her husband, Mark, joined the Church in 2006. They have three sons and a daughter. Lisa would love to find more time to read and paint.

His Promises Are Sure

BY LUCY EKANEM

TO THE READERS OF MY TESTIMONY, if you are in doubt of the truth, God has a way to guide you on the right path.

I am grateful He gave me the opportunity and paved the way for me to be in America in quest of education. That quest has led me to a more meaningful path—the gospel of Jesus Christ.

It started when a young girl who had a boyfriend serving a mission in South Africa met me on the University of Utah campus and introduced herself to me through small talk. I must admit I was not very receptive of her initially, but she persisted with kindness. She invited me to Relief Society events to talk about my culture, to dinner with her family, to Mormon Tabernacle Choir concerts, and to the temple open house in West Jordan, Utah, in 1981. The friendship continued after my graduation, even when I left Utah for Minnesota. I still did not join the Church, but my two older children were baptized in Utah.

THE HAND OF THE LORD

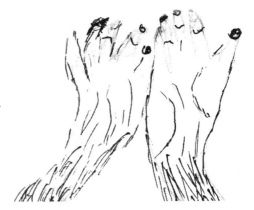

I drew this picture of hands to remind me that Jesus Christ has carved me, and all of us, on the palms of His hands.

I finally submitted to baptism on January 30, 1988. These words, based on Isaiah 49:16, "See! I will not forget you...I have carved you on the palms of my hands," are on the bookmark a sister gave me on the day of my baptism. I have a testimony that God knows every one of us as well as our needs. I have come to understanding that He speaks to us through the scriptures, based from the one of this bookmark. Little did I understand the power of His love then, but through the Atonement of the Savior, He has carved me on the palms of His hands. In other words, Heavenly Father was telling me, I was on the right track to begin my mortal journey after my baptism.

I have experienced and seen countless blessings from God since my membership. Nevertheless, I have faced many trials that could have taken me down to the dust. But through those trials, I have learned to trust Him as long as I keep my baptismal covenant. I have come to realize that those trials are for my own good to shape me like fine gold. I have come to appreciate the sufferings of the Savior to atone for my sins. I am grateful for the knowledge and the hope that Heavenly Father sent to me through this scripture after my baptism.

Lucy Ekanem was born in Calabar, in the state of Cross River, Nigeria. In 1978 she moved to Utah to pursue an education. She graduated from the University of Utah and in 1984 moved to Minnesota to obtain a graduate degree in business finance from the University of Minnesota. She was baptized in 1988 and later received her endowments in the Chicago Temple, being sealed to her parents, Nkoyo Inyang and Essien Ekanem, on the same day. She has five children and one grandchild. Lucy has a passion for volunteerism, reading, and traveling to see natural wonders such as Old Faithful in Wyoming. She also enjoys visiting Church history sites.

Have pity upon me, have pity upon me, O ye my friends; for the hand of God hath touched me.
Job 19:21

The Unlikely Convert

BY NANCY GAYDER

IT WAS AN OVERCAST, CHILLING DAY late in December as the afternoon sun was trying to nuzzle its way through the clouds. I lay on my bed, cigarette in one hand and a whiskey shot in the other. It was a lazy day and I was contemplating my life. I was 33 years old and wanted more out of life.

I had a full-time job as an accounting team leader, was extremely active in the Presbyterian church as an elder, superintendent of the Sunday School, co-leader of the junior, junior high, senior high and college groups and other groups as necessary. Busy 24/7, yet it wasn't enough. Something was still missing. But what?

I had been in bed about three hours when I heard a knock on my door downstairs. As I got there, I saw two impeccably dressed young men—white shirts, ties, suit, the whole shot! A total GQ look. They had come to teach me about their church, the true church, The Church of Jesus Christ of Latter-day Saints, the Mormons! They were full-time missionaries of the Church. Now if there is anything that I love, it's a challenge. I invited them in and we got down to business. They with their King James scriptures, me with my twelve various translations!

It was an exhilarating afternoon. I began to have them over twice a week, serving dinner first and then studying. I refused to pray about the truthfulness of their church. If I didn't pray, I wouldn't have to take any action. My friends had provided me with all the anti-Mormon literature they could possibly find.

During sacrament meeting I always sat between the two missionaries about five rows back from the front. Sacrament was always given at the early part of the meeting, with bread first, then water. After I selected my piece of bread, I would lean forward and speak with my Heavenly Father, then scoot back, sit up straight and wait for the water. At this particular meeting, staying true to form I selected my bread, partook of it and leaned forward to again pray in love and gratitude. In that prayer, I *accidentally* prayed about the truthfulness of the Church. My answer came loud and clear. I felt the answer must have been audible, but I had no proof. I instantly sat bolt upright on the bench, as did the two missionaries. They looked at each other, looked at me, and grinned. "You prayed, didn't you?" They had also received my answer and knew instantly that now I knew. The three of us continued sitting there, grins on our faces, being totally joyful and full of thanksgiving and praise. I had prayed for the truth and had been given the answer, so now I had to act on it.

On May 1, 1980, I was baptized into The Church of Jesus Christ of Latter-day Saints and was confirmed. My old life was now behind me and ahead of me stretched a new journey into the true Church and its teachings—a way for a much better life and closeness with my Heavenly Father. The missionaries brought me to the truth, and I found the missing pieces of my life.

Nancy Gayder passed away on May 2, 2013, while this book was in production. Before her last illness she contributed this story and one other. She was a member of the Apple Valley Ward less than two years and made many new friends here while retaining close ties with friends in the Farmington Ward. Nancy was born in St. Paul, Minnesota, the daughter of Kenneth and Edith Dunn. She joined the Church in 1980. Before her retirement she worked as an accountant in an insurance firm. She loved people, dogs, crossword puzzles, and Disney movies. Because of her last name, she also liked to collect things with an alligator motif.

A Constant Guide

by Tonia Gintz

THE PAST FEW YEARS it feels as if the Lord's hand has been constantly guiding me, gently providing opportunities for me. It all started on a relatively ordinary Tuesday evening in October of 2009 when two impeccably dressed young men knocked at my door. I was a single mom of three young children who were very distracting, so I don't remember much about what we talked about that first night, but I do remember telling them that I already attended church and that I was active and happy in my church. They asked if they could share a message anyway and I agreed since I rarely pass up an opportunity to learn more about other faiths and cultures. We set an appointment for the missionaries to come back two days later. I spent the next two days wondering why on earth I had invited them back! What could possibly come of this meeting?

On Thursday evening, I was thinking, "Maybe they forgot about our appointment. Maybe they just won't come back." No such luck! Those boys were right on time! They arrived at precisely 7 p.m., the agreed upon meeting hour, and I led them into my little living room. They began with telling me a little about who they were and why they were there. They asked me who my favorite prophet was. I only hesitated a moment before answering "Jeremiah" which they took as an interesting, yet valid answer. If only they knew he was the only prophet I could think of, and I could only think of him because I heard the Protestant song "Jeremiah was a Prophet" sung to the tune of "Jeremiah was a Bullfrog" in my head, they would have either laughed at me or shaken their heads with pity. They explained to me that ancient people had come to America before Christopher Columbus and that Jesus Christ had shown up here, too. Oh, and by the way, there's a prophet on the earth today! *Yeah, right!* I was pretty skeptical, but continued to listen politely. It wasn't until Elder Steel bore testimony of the truthfulness of the Book of Mormon and of the gospel that I had any inclination to invite them back. During his testimony, I could *feel* the power of his words. It was like there was electricity sparking around the room. I thought to myself, "Who on earth is this kid? And how can someone so young be *so* sure of anything, when I'm ten years older than him and am sure of nothing?" I wanted to know more about what was making these boys so happy and so confident. They invited me to accept a copy of the Book of Mormon and asked if I would read it and pray regarding its truthfulness. I agreed and we set another appointment for them to return the following week.

I began reading the book that night and found I didn't want to stop! It seemed familiar to me somehow, like I already knew how the story would go even though I didn't know anything about this guy Nephi (pronounced "Neh-fee" in my head until I discovered the pronunciation guide at the back of the book and sheepishly corrected myself). I found it similar to the Bible, but different somehow and not only because it was about different characters and different stories than those that I remembered from the Bible. When the elders came back, they asked me how my reading and prayer had been going. When I told them how much I had read, they seemed shocked. I later learned that it's because these wonderful young men were so accustomed to hearing that the person "forgot" to read or had only read a page or two before giving up. I told them that I hadn't really been doing very well at the praying part of the deal though. I was kind of embarrassed to admit that I was 30 years old and felt like I didn't know how to pray. They were more than willing to help me learn. That night before going to bed, I got down on my knees for the first time since I was a little kid praying "Now I lay me down to sleep..." and said probably the first truly heartfelt prayer of my life. I wasn't struck by lightning; there was no "Aha!" moment, no glorious revelations. Instead, I fell asleep almost instantly.

The next morning, I awoke feeling fabulous. The sun seemed brighter, the sky bluer, and the birds cheerier! Several of my co-workers even commented on my good mood. I had been at work for a couple of hours when it finally dawned on me—*I knew!* The joy I felt inside me was confirmation from the Holy Spirit that the Book of Mormon was true. I felt as if I might burst with love and joy that day. I couldn't wait to get home and tell the elders that *I knew!* I was so excited to speak to them again and so excited to read more and learn more. Elder Steel says he will never forget that day when I held up the Book of Mormon and said, "I know this is true!" I still needed to gain a testimony of a living prophet, but my faith was growing, though I was not patient with myself. I remember asking myself, "Do you believe that Noah built a boat and sailed an ark full of animals around until the mountaintop dried?" Yes, I did. "Well, then why couldn't Nephi build a boat to sail to another continent?" Point taken. "Do you believe that God spoke to Moses?" Yes, I did. "Well, then why is it so hard to believe that God could speak to Joseph Smith? Why is it so hard to believe in a living prophet?" The answer was simple. "I don't know. I guess I need to have faith." The elders read the thirty-second chapter of Alma with me and I felt empowered. The verses in Alma 32:26-36 were pivotal to my conversion. I realized that I didn't need to have a perfect knowledge of it all. It didn't need to make perfect sense. I just needed to open my heart and let the truth in and give it some space for a while. I did just that. I let the gospel into my heart and it grew.

I once heard a story about a lamp salesman that completely reminds me of myself when I was first introduced to the gospel. In the story, a lamp salesman knocked on a door and tried to sell a lamp to the man that lived there. The man said, "But I already have a lamp. See? I don't need your lamp." The lamp salesman said, "Sir, just let me show you my lamp and if you don't like it I will go away." The lamp salesman was admitted to the home where he proceeded to plug in his lamp. The lamp shone so brightly that it dispelled the gloom and illuminated all corners of the room. The homeowner was amazed. He had never seen a lamp so glorious and so bright. He hadn't known what he was missing living in his gloomy house. He was able to clearly see things that he'd never seen before. Now that he had seen the light, he knew that he needed it in his life. I was that skeptical man from the story.

I hadn't known what I was missing because I had never had it in my life. Once I got a taste of the gospel, I knew that I couldn't live without it! I progressed rapidly and was baptized within six weeks of meeting the missionaries.

Just over a month later, there was a stake singles activity in Lakeville, and I hadn't really even thought about going. I didn't think I was really ready to start a relationship with anybody and didn't think that this event would be of any interest to me. A friend from my ward said, "You're going. I'll pick you up at 12:15." So I went. I wasn't going to argue with her. We arrived slightly early, so I was watching the guys set up the tables. A particular guy caught my attention as being kind of cute, and before long he came over to our table to ask someone to say the opening prayer. Being a new member, I had not yet mastered the avoidance of eye contact when the person conducting is looking for someone to say a prayer. So, he looked right at me and asked me if I would mind offering the prayer. I remember saying, "I've only been a member for a month!" But everyone at my table encouraged me, so I agreed. Not many words were exchanged with this man who was looking for someone to pray—just first names and which wards we were from. The rest of that day passed pretty uneventfully.

Just over a week later, I was googling something beginning with LDS, and LDS Mingle popped up in the suggestion box. I clicked on it just out of curiosity and found I could fill out a free profile and see my matches. Oh, what the heck. I gave it a try just for giggles. I finished filling out my profile and clicked submit and four guys popped up as a "100% Match" for me. One of those four was the man that I had met at the singles event mere days earlier! I sent him one of the free messages that pretty much said, "Hey, I like your profile" and soon was rewarded with an email from him. I then realized that although the profile was free, I would have to pay for the service to read the emails. Grrr. I wasn't that interested in dating! I wasn't going to pay some fee to read an email. A few days later, I got another email from this gentleman. Darn! Curiosity had me in its clutches! I signed up for the service because I *had* to read those emails. It's a good thing I did, or I would have missed out on the biggest blessing of my life. That man is now my wonderful husband. We were sealed in the temple and have recently added a new baby to our blended family.

One could look at the events in my life over the last few years and pass them off as mere coincidences, but I know better. The hand of the Lord has been in my life since the beginning. I just didn't realize it until now. Everything that I've gone through in my life has made me who I am today. My trials have strengthened me and taught me important lessons. The Lord prepared me to hear the gospel. He gave me a thirst for knowledge so that I would be intrigued by what the elders had to offer. He even made sure our paths crossed. I normally had an ECFE [Early Childhood and Family Education] class on Tuesday evenings, but for some reason we did not go to ECFE that day. The kids and I were just hanging out at home apparently waiting for the missionaries to find us. I fully believe that every convert has his/her "own" missionary or missionaries. The missionaries that I met were just the ones that the Lord knew would connect with me in a powerful way. Wonderful people were introduced into my life to help me along my path including several amazing members from the ward. My husband, Jeff, hadn't wanted to go to the singles event that day, but had been asked to conduct so was obligated to attend. I hadn't wanted to go but was urged by friends. Then Jeff was selected from a nationwide database of Latter-day Saints on the LDS Mingle site as a match for me. It was all too perfectly orchestrated to be mere coincidence. I know that my Heavenly Father loves me and knows me individually. He knows what is best for me and gives me opportunities when the time is right. I just need to have faith and listen for the voice of the Spirit.

Recently I was privileged to witness the baptism of my oldest daughter from my first marriage. Her father was in attendance and she was baptized by her stepfather. I believe that Heavenly Father had a hand in helping my ex-husband accept the choices of an 8-year-old and allow her to be baptized. A few weeks later I was privileged to witness the blessing of my youngest daughter. She is a beautiful gift from Heavenly Father, as are all my children. I thank Heavenly Father for the sweet spirits that He has entrusted me with. My firm testimony is that the hand of the Lord is with us, helping us and guiding us at all times. We can look back at crucial points in our lives and recognize His work. I pray that I will always be open to His gentle guidance.

Tonia Gintz was born in Blue Earth, Minnesota, and is the daughter of Mark D. and Ruth A. Green. She joined the Church in 2009 in Mankato, Minnesota, and moved to the Apple Valley Ward following her marriage a year later. She and her husband, Jeff, have a blended family of six children. She loves nature photography but for the time being has switched to taking pictures of her family. She also loves to read classic novels, but her favorite thing of all right now would be to take a long, hot bubble bath with no children knocking on the door.

What I've Learned Along the Way

BY DIANNE ANDERSON

IT WAS A TYPICAL DAY at work with four of us working in the front office as the morning and afternoon shifts overlapped during the lunch hour. The front door opened unexpectedly. Busy with my paperwork, I remember looking up into the smiling faces of two young men in white shirts, ties, and name tags.

My boss came out from his office and welcomed them with warm greetings and handshakes. After a brief introduction, the three of them disappeared into the back office. Without giving it any more thought, I let myself get absorbed back into my work. A while later I was surprised to see my boss come back, alone, to the counter where we were working. Silently staring at us all for a second he said, "If any of you know what's good for you, you'll go talk to these guys!"

I was the only one he was able to convince to go back to his office where these two mysterious young men were waiting. I was nervous. What in the world was I going to say? However, the Spirit did all the talking. In fact, as soon as I entered the room I remember feeling embraced by some kind of warmth and, as I sat down, they began to talk. They didn't get very far before the tears leapt from my eyes. And that's how it went for the next half hour or so. They talked, I wept. I went to church the next Sunday and have never looked back.

Next month I celebrate thirty-two years of the new path that day put me on. It changed how I lived my life, how I raised my kids, how I see *everything*. What an amazing perspective one can have when given the knowledge of who they really are! I don't know how I would have made it through the deep and painful valleys of my life without this incredible understanding.

Here's what I've learned along the way:

1) *Miracles DO happen*! The first was when I received permission from my non-member ex-husband to have my son baptized, followed by an even more miraculous granting of permission four years later to have him sealed to me! That miracle was the icing on the cake of another huge miracle—finding my daughter, through adoption: it was a long process that involved forms, interviews, doctor appointments, meetings, more interviews, and more forms. We met every month or so with the LDS social worker who would bring us data sheets of children who were up for adoption. From the beginning I had a deep feeling that I would *know* my child when the paperwork was in front of me. One day in June, about three years after we'd begun these meetings, he showed up with two data sheets, both for babies that had not been born yet but would be placed for adoption after their births. As I stared at these papers, one in each hand, I heard myself say, "This one is going to be a boy," as I waved the paper in my left hand, and then

waving the one in my right hand, "And this one is going to be a girl. And she's *ours!*" Both statements turned out to be true.

2) *The Holy Ghost will help you in very real and amazing ways.* I have heard its *many* whisperings: as a Young Women's leader being warned to move my girls to safety while at camp during a mild rainstorm, and finding our camp leveled the next morning when we came out from the emergency shelter; as a worn and weary Relief Society president being instructed specifically what was left for me to do in the calling before I would be released; as a teacher in numerous settings being stopped from continuing my carefully planned lesson because someone in the room needed to hear something else; as a tired mom and wife driving home after work and being warned to move to a different lane of traffic on an empty road late at night, and being saved moments later from a head-on collision with a car speeding around a bend in the road on the wrong side of the highway.

3) *There IS a God, and even better, turns out we're related!* I am the child of a loving Father in Heaven, whose reality and existence is emblazoned on my heart from countless times on my knees speaking to Him as easily as to an earthly father and feeling His presence—especially in my darkest hours, as though his arms were literally wrapped around me. It is my greatest desire to return home to Him!

4) *Jesus IS the Christ.* He not only suffered for every wrong choice I have made, but also endured every pain, sickness, and sorrow I have felt or will yet experience. His sacrifice has taught me humility, tolerance, deep gratitude, and a purer way to love. For me, the real journey of this life is fueled by the desire to understand as well as I can the many layers of this unspeakable gift.

5) *The Book of Mormon IS scripture.* I know because I've read from its pages almost every day for the last three decades. I have felt the witness of the Holy Ghost countless times as I've read, studied, and pondered the word of God from the Bible as well as the Book of Mormon. I still use my original set of scriptures, even though they are falling apart, because they have become a dear companion that I can't bear to be separated from.

6) *Prayer is almost too good to be true!* I had prayed as a child and with much less frequency as an adult, but it was not until the missionaries taught me that I realized who I was speaking to and then learned the incredible fact that I could expect *answers*—that He would actually speak back! This is an immeasurable gift, in my opinion.

7) *The Church is TRUE.* There is no denying the facts: I have felt literally all my life that there is a "right" way to do things. Where could that be more true than with a perfect Father in Heaven, who is the epitome of order and exactness? I grew up believing that if Jesus Christ were on the earth there would be one way of doing things—His way. I just didn't know what that was, exactly, because it was never the same. I wanted to be "happy" like the born-again Christians I knew and devout like the Catholics who were my friends, but nowhere did I find anything that told me it was right, until that day in the office, sitting across the desk from two unfamiliar men who told me things that were deeply familiar.

8) *To top this all off, the most precious possessions in my life are ones I get to keep FOREVER: my family!* THIS is the good news of the gospel for me, that there is a plan in place and that we are all

part of a marvelous story that has the ending we all dream of, that of being together forever.

I once asked Heavenly Father (in prayer) why it took so long for Him to send the missionaries to find me. I was annoyed so much of my life had been "wasted." I was clearly told that it was because *I* wasn't ready. He'd been watching all along.

Dianne Anderson was living in Bemidji, Minnesota, when she was baptized in 1981. As a new member, she was immediately called into the Young Women's program and has served in many capacities since then. She has lived in the Apple Valley Ward since 2009. She was born in Langdon, North Dakota; her parents are Donald O. and Norma A. Anderson. She holds an associate degree in accounting. She loves self-help books and workshops, especially in the field of natural healing. She has two married children and six amazing grandchildren.

Unshackled

BY CAITLIN ROBINSON

THE BEST WAY I can share my testimony is to share a bit about my conversion: my life before I found the Church, how I came to know the Church, and my life after baptism.

Before I found the Church, I was simply lost. I was half-heartedly trudging through life. I knew that I desperately longed for change and freedom from my pain and frustration. I was incredibly overwhelmed. Where do I even begin to fix the mess that I've made of my life? I didn't fully realize then, but I was operating under two very incorrect notions: 1) God has given up on me. 2) My life will never get any better.

When I needed it most, God gave me proof that He had not and will not give up on me. He did so by bringing two of His divine tools into my life in the form of two missionaries—Elder Walker and Elder Walls. When I was at my breaking point, they showed up at my door. They came looking to speak with my mother, whom they met earlier in the week. As luck would have it, they met me instead.

So there I was, standing in the doorway listening to two complete strangers testify of their belief in the gospel. Normally when a missionary of some sort would come to my door, I would politely listen to the typical spiel and never give it another thought after they left. I've had plenty of folks come to my door claiming to believe in one god or another, but these two seemed different. They were nice people, but they also carried the Spirit with them. From then on, it snowballed from my being curious about this religion into needing to know how these two got the privilege of having the Holy Spirit with them. I wanted that presence in my life too.

My conversion has been swift and to the point. God knew what He wanted for my life, and I jumped in with both feet. I have learned so much about the Church and the gospel, involved myself in every way I can at the church, and took the big step—getting baptized. I think that's the best way. Just take the leap of faith, and know that if you at least try to follow Him, He won't let you fall.

I can safely say that my life is changing for the better. That's not to say that my struggles have disappeared since being baptized, but at least now I know that I am not alone in them. The important thing to remember is that Satan may have his hand on your shoulder sometimes, but God always has His hand on your heart.

I've met many wonderful people, learned infinite truths, and felt indescribable amounts of blessings and comfort. I know that a big reason for all of this is because God has a plan for me, and the elders were willing tools of God. That is something that I now strive to be every day: a willing tool of God.

Since joining the church I have been reminded of a few immutable facts that I feel obliged to share: 1) The past is not somewhere that God dwells, and neither should you. 2) God does not punish; He teaches. 3) "If He brings you to it, He will bring you through it."

Until I found the Church, I was existing in a prison that Satan built and I maintained. I am now living because God has unshackled me and brought me into His light. For this blessing I am eternally grateful. I testify that Heavenly Father and Jesus Christ live and love us, Joseph Smith is a prophet, we are led today by a living prophet, and The Church of Jesus Christ of Latter-day Saints is the Savior's Church restored on the earth.

Caitlin Robinson moved to Minnesota about thirteen years ago. She was born in Grand Rapids, Michigan, and is the daughter of Rix Robinson and Kari Ann Buckley. She joined the Church in 2013 and was immediately called to serve in the Relief Society. She currently works at a collision repair shop in Minneapolis and plans to eventually own and operate an inn. She enjoys arts and crafts, photography, cooking, and country music.

Changing Points in My Life

BY FRANCES MARIE DAVIS

WHEN I WAS YOUNG I used to drink. It didn't bother me any. I was working at the main post office and I could do more work drunk than most people could do sober. I could keep a bottle of liquor right there in my work station, and they knew it and they allowed it, because it kept me from wandering around and bothering people. I had friends all over the building and I would go talk to them. So I would sit there and sort mail to go to all the different states.

One night I heard a voice—I don't know who it was. (At that time I didn't have a relationship with God. Sometimes I think now I don't have a relationship with Him; that is, I talk to Him, but He don't say nothing back.) I do know now He loves me. I heard a voice say as clear as day that if I did not stop drinking I would not live out the year. So I got up immediately and went to the main office and asked for a transfer to another station.

I got my transfer and went to a post office on 125th Street in Manhattan. Even though there were bars and clubs and liquor all around, and lots of famous restaurants—if you wanted to drink, there was liquor everywhere—but I didn't give into the urge. I stayed away from that stuff. Somehow I just changed. So that was the end of that period of my life. I don't know why it happened, but I'm glad it did. That was one of the deciding moments in my life.

The second deciding moment in my life was when I went to South Carolina in January 2003 to care for my dad. He had Alzheimer's and we didn't know it. At first it would come and go, and then it just came and stayed. My mother had passed away in 1980 with bone cancer. My dad had remarried and moved to South Carolina. Even though we went to see him three times a year, my stepmother had her family around and she wasn't happy having us around, so we had to stay at a hotel. Then my stepmother died and she had been dead over a year and we didn't know it. He didn't know he was supposed to tell anybody.

So that's when I retired and went to take care of him. That's when I met my first Mormon sisters, Sister Jessica Poole and Sister Ruth (I don't know her first name). The first Mormons I'd ever met. We didn't have Mormons going door to door there in New York at that time, and we didn't have a temple in New York either.

The sisters were being kind to my dad because he was there by himself and they knew he needed help. They didn't know who to contact. He would get Meals on Wheels but he didn't know to thaw the food out. He would try to eat it frozen. And he would be out walking and they would find him and take him back home and sit with him until they could get someone to come and get him.

So when I met them, I was amazed that people could be so nice when there was nothing in it for them. I had no family in South Carolina. They were being kind to me also because I didn't know anyone there. (The last thing I expected was to end up in South Carolina. I was not a South Carolina girl.) I had never met anyone that genuinely honest. They asked me if they could give me lessons and come by and visit. There was just me and my father, who I called "my little Fruit Loop," so I said yes and that's how I was introduced to the Church.

I started going to church with them and there were so many nice people there in the church where they took me. They were the nicest people I'd ever met in my life. When you got to the door, there were people standing there greeting you and telling you how nice it was for you to be there. One family there, Brother Hall and his wife, had adopted four children from Russia. He was always asking me to come to Sunday dinner with his family, but I would make up all excuses and out and out lie to keep from going because I was afraid I would be out of my element.

One day he said (this was Brother Hall), he said, "If you don't come to my house, I'm going to come and get you." I said, "Well I have to make dinner for my dad." He said, "We'll take care of Dad. Don't worry about it." He and his wife would invite four and five families for dinner on Sunday, so I got there and the bishop was there and other families, and they had this giant table. It reminded me of those long tables in medieval castles where twenty people could sit. The Halls went out of their way to make me feel comfortable. When I left, they gave me dinner for Dad, and they loaded me up with a bunch of other goodies for my dad too.

There were so many nice people there, it changed my whole personality. It changed the way I thought, it changed me. I knew I wanted to be a better person. I knew I wanted to have a better life. It was just nice to meet people and not have your guard up. That's when I decided to be baptized, and that's another whole story.

The sisters taught me how to pray. They had this little book for people who don't know how to pray, and it told you this is how you're supposed to do it.

Another thing that helped me decide about joining the Church was going to a fireside chat at the stake center in Charleston, South Carolina, in 2003. Daniel Rona gave the talk. He grew up in New York as a Jew and he converted to being a Mormon. His whole talk was relevant to me because I grew up in New York and I knew exactly what he was saying and where he was talking about. When I listened to him, it was like walking over steps in my life. It was so real. I grew up in a Jewish household in a Jewish community. (When you're a child, you follow your parents' lead. You believe what they believe, but when you grow up, you develop ideas of your own.) What he said was very touching for me, so at the end I went up to talk to him and tell him that it had made me feel close to him. He gave me a CD of his talk.

My family was surprised and I think a little annoyed when I joined the Church. I have cousins in California who are atheists and they were put out with me. But I didn't ask their permission. I didn't ask anyone's permission. This was for me. It wasn't about them and I was happy with it.

A year after I joined the Church, I went to the temple in Columbia, South Carolina. The missionaries who had been with me and helped me all along, they all showed up. My best friend was there too. (That is, the sisters had introduced me to her at church and we had become best friends.) I didn't know they were coming. I had no clue. It was one of most beautiful and nicest things that ever happened in my life, for people to give their time and come all that way. It was a trip, it wasn't like going next door.

It's been a good life since I joined the Church. I'm glad for the change. I've been happy.

Frances Marie Davis was born in Williamston, North Carolina, the daughter of Horace and Alease Slade Davis, but she grew up in New York City. She raised her daughter, Cindy, as a single parent and worked for the United States Postal Service for thirty-eight years. She retired to South Carolina in 2003, where she joined the Church. She moved to Minnesota in 2006 so she could help care for her grandson, David, who is "Grandma's boy."

My Story

BY DIANE JOHNSON

MY STORY STARTS IN THE MID 1980S when my husband and I joined the Church. I had known about the LDS Church for a long time because my brother had joined when he was 17. I had been raised in the Presbyterian church. We received the missionary lessons from two angelic sister missionaries who had the Spirit about them in every way. We joined the Church just before my husband, who was in the Army, was re-assigned from a base in North Carolina to being an Army Recruiter in a small town in Wisconsin. Most people there had never met a Mormon, and the ones who knew about the Church were praying for us because they thought we were members of a cult.

The small branch we belonged to was over an hour's drive away. There were only about twenty members, and when one family moved out, there were only about twelve. To say the least, our new standing in the Church was compromised by distance, three young children, and not really being able to see how the organization worked when there weren't enough members. My husband was not committed enough to ensure that the kids went to church, so for the next six years the kids and I went to the Lutheran church in town. I figured that some church was better than no church at all.

During this time we reverted to some old behaviors. I began smoking again and my husband continued with his drinking problems. We weren't doing well as a family; something was missing, but I just didn't get it yet. Then we got orders to go to Europe. Somehow, crazy as it sounds, I thought that moving to Germany would heal our wounds and we would be a better family.

My middle daughter was in third grade. She had a teacher at the Department of Defense School who had a rabbit in her classroom. She was kind and gentle with the children and just had a sort of glow about her. I have since learned to recognize this in people who are members of the Church but I didn't know what it was at that time. My daughter adored her and I spent many hours volunteering in her class. Eventually I got a job in the DOD school as a substitute teacher because this teacher recommended me. We became good friends. Her name was Sharon.

After being in Germany for about six months, I felt it was really time to get back to church. I found that our military ward in Germany was quite large. The first event we attended was a Pioneer Day picnic. As we walked through all the festivities, I saw Sharon in the crowd. She ran to me and embraced me and asked if I was a member of the Church. I told her I was. She immediately began to apologize because the Spirit had been prompting her to invite me to church and she had not acted on the prompting.

We then became friends on a whole other level. She kept my ration card under lock and key so that I could quit smoking.

(Cigarettes, tea, and coffee were only available to us in the military stores with a ration card.) We became active in the ward and made many new friends. It was during this time that my three kids were baptized by their father. He did his best to be a solid priesthood holder, but it was hard for him.

It was in the middle of the Gulf War and a trying time for military members overseas. As time passed, the culture shock of living so far from home, the war, and many other factors were tearing our family apart. It eventually became just the kids and me going to church again. My husband began to drink again. My friend Sharon and other families in the ward helped us through some very difficult times.

The kids and I returned to the States before my husband did. The marriage ended in divorce, but I did my best to follow the commandments. It was at this time in my life that I realized that we cannot get anyone into the temple but ourselves. We are all responsible for our own eternal salvation. I went through a few very troubled years, raising my kids on my own and trying my best to keep it all together and get everyone to church. After a time I was finally ready to go to the temple. Sharon's family had also returned stateside, and they lived in a small town in Illinois.

My brother traveled to Minnesota to escort me to the Chicago Temple. My friend Sharon traveled to Chicago and met us there. They both escorted me through the temple for the first time. Sharon gave me a temple apron to remember my first time in the temple. Each time I wear it I think of her. Had it not been for her, I am not sure I would have remained active in the Church.

Many years have passed since then. I remarried a wonderful man and had him for nine years. He wasn't a member of the

Church, but supported me and the Church completely. He gave me and my children many precious gifts that money can't buy. He died quite suddenly a few years ago. Some dear friends in the Church escorted me to the temple a year after he died. I was sealed to him for all time and eternity that day.

I learned through these experiences that we should live our lives so that we can hear promptings of the Spirit, that I will never again live without a temple recommend, and that I will always remember that the smallest things you do can have a huge impact in someone else's life.

Diane Johnson loves hiking and spending time in nature, which explains why she thoroughly enjoyed her calling as Young Women camp director for several years. She also likes sewing but spends most of her fun time with her five grandchildren. She was born in Minneapolis, the daughter of Donald and Mitzi Hadd, and was baptized in 1984 in Fayetteville, North Carolina. Diane has an associate degree in nursing and works as a nurse in an intensive care unit. She was a stay-at-home mom when her three children were young.

My Search Began in Sixth Grade

BY JACQUELYN A. KELLINGTON

THE ORANGE CRATE was just the right size. Mom had a piece of purple velvet that would cover most of it, and I could easily make room for it in my closet. My sister Sandy thought I was a bit crazy. But I took seriously that part in the scriptures that tells us to pray in our closets, and so I created an altar in my closet, a place to pray.

I was in the sixth grade, and at that time we had many opportunities to attend Bible classes. Our school, Longfellow Elementary, even allowed students to leave early once a week to attend Bible study if they chose to do so. An elderly lady who lived across the street from the school invited any children who were interested to come into her home for Bible discussions. I loved going there. I looked forward to the Bible stories she would share. I was excited to feel that one day I would be able to meet the Jesus we talked so much about.

She explained to me, however, that we would never actually meet Him or see Him because He didn't have a body like ours. But she enthusiastically explained to me His greatness. He was so big He filled the universe, yet He was so small He could dwell in my heart. He could be everywhere at the same time. I was confused and disappointed. I didn't understand. How was I to love someone who was really neither here nor there and just everywhere?

I tried to make sense of it. I really did. But I had questions. What of Gethsemane? Was He praying to Himself? I questioned the crucifixion. What did the nails pierce if not a body? And what of His resurrection, was it not a body that was resurrected? And then didn't He show the nail prints in His hands to people?

For some time I remained interested in religion even in my confusion, but then I became a teenager and my interest took a swing in another direction. After some time I met my husband-to-be. Chuck and I dated for nearly three years and were married. Into our marriage came three children, the youngest of whom was Barbie, who was mentally handicapped.

My interest in religion began again to occupy a part of my mind. I, however, was still confused about the Godhead. My mother had recently joined a church. With great clarity she explained the Godhead as it was taught in the Restoration. Her words made sense and I was interested, but the business of my life kept me from pursuing it.

At the age of 1, my daughter Barbie developed strep throat, pneumonia, German measles, and croup all at the same time. My mother, who was serving as Relief Society president at the time, sent two priesthood holders from the Church to the hospital to administer to my daughter. They returned and reported to my mother that Barbie was a special spirit and had an important work to do. She would complete it at a very young age and would not be required to tarry on the earth for a long time. I won't go into the details of her death here but will simply say that she drowned at the age of 6.

I was, of course, anguished, and after a time a sort of numbness set in, masking somewhat the pain. After Barbie's burial I simply had to know where she was. I had dreams of looking and searching for Barbie. I recall one dream where I was flying like a bird over the world searching, searching, and not finding her. I couldn't accept what some told me—that she was just gone, the grave was an ending, and she was really not anywhere. They said that she wasn't suffering because when we die that is the end. Some told me that, for my peace of mind, I needed to accept that existence is only earthly. But I could not accept it.

Mom knew better and sent two sister missionaries to visit me. I was hurting so much I was willing to listen to any and all explanations. Besides, I trusted my mom and recalled some of the things she had told me that had felt right.

The sister missionaries spoke of a Restoration, explaining that many precious truths had been lost or misinterpreted. They shared with me prophets from the Bible who spoke of other records, records that would come forth in the latter days. They said that the Bible and the Book of Mormon together would make clear for me where my Barbie was.

Also, how clear was their explanation of the Godhead. How simple. It made sense, and knowing that the day would come when I would see both the Father and the Son as two separate personages gave me a sense of peace and excitement. I just knew it was true. I could feel it!

Jackie Kellington, age 30, soon after she joined the Church.

And Barbie—I would be reunited with her. I learned that she was living in the presence of the Father, the Father of her spirit with whom she once dwelled, as did we all before our earthly entrance. The plan was familiar; it was as if it was all coming back to me. I knew. I just knew the sister missionaries were messengers speaking truth—the truth I was ready for, the truth that opened my understanding, releasing me from the pain of my Barbie's death and answering with clarity questions of long ago, questions I had even as a sixth grader. It was like a lightbulb flashing in my head. I was asked to pray about the message the sisters brought me. I didn't feel I needed to, but I did, and the burning in my being was my confirmation.

During my teenage years I had picked up a nasty habit. At that time it was cool to smoke. I became so addicted that I lit up a cigarette before answering the phone. I kept a lit cigarette on the edge of the tub while I was bathing. My habit was very strong. I had tried many times to quit, but to no avail. Chuck urged me continually to quit, also to no avail.

The sister missionaries wanted to set a date for my baptism. The date they suggested was only two weeks away! I wanted to be baptized, I truly did, but how was I ever going to be able to overcome such a strong addiction? At the very moment they were asking me to confirm the date, I was craving a cigarette. But I wanted this religion more than anything. I agreed to the date. We knelt in prayer. Upon arising, the sisters asked me for my cigarettes. I remember thinking, "What? I thought I'd have two weeks to work on my addiction!" Besides, I had just purchased a carton, something I rarely did because of the expense. I almost wished they had asked me for my arm, not my cigarettes. But I wanted this, and I knew I needed to exercise faith. I gave them my carton of cigarettes. When the girls left, closing the door, to my amazement and gratitude, my habit went with them, or rather, the Lord took my habit. I believe He knew I was not able to do it alone. How many times had I tried to quit? Many. I can and do testify to this amazing miracle for which I am grateful. Never ever have I had a desire for one of those horrific things since the door closed in that small apartment years ago.

With every facet of my being I know the Bible and the Book of Mormon are true and that I will finally see this Jesus face-to-face, a search that I began long ago, even as a sixth grader.

Jacquelyn A. Kellington has a gift for meeting people and learning how special they are. She was born in Minneapolis, Minnesota, and joined the Church in 1963. She has served in many callings, including being a stake missionary and a temple ordinance worker. She is a trained dental surgery assistant and recognizes God's hand in directing her to this profession. She also worked as a certified foster care provider for hard to place children and as a nanny for many years. She developed a deep love for the children she cared for. Jackie and her husband, Chuck, have six children of their own. Her parents are John Russel and Hannah Morehead Hoffman.

*Behold, I will lead thee by the hand,
and I will take thee, to put upon thee my name.
Abraham 1:18*

Our Daughter
Led the Way

BY NORMA E. STORLAND

This story is reprinted from The Gift of Love: A Mormon Women's Journal, *published in 1982 by the Minneapolis Minnesota Stake Relief Society. That book became the inspiration for this one, just as Norma's life continues to be an inspiration for all of us.*

MY MOST SPIRITUAL EXPERIENCE would be the baptisms of my husband and me in June 1980. We had been members of a Lutheran church in our area for thirty-two years. Our daughter Janet found the Church in 1976, and in 1977 our married daughter Judy was baptized in Norway. In 1978 we supported Janet on her mission to Norway.

In her many letters we gained a lot of spiritual knowledge, and when we went to Norway to visit our married daughter, we were able to visit with Janet.

We promised when we returned home we would take the discussions, which we did in the spring of 1980. We were challenged to set a date and we did for June 28, 1980. Our teenage son attended our baptism and was so moved by the Holy Ghost that he took the lessons and was baptized by his father on July 28, 1980.

It has been a very rewarding two years as our son is now in the Philippines on a mission. Before he left, we were able to go through the temple in Mesa, Arizona, and be sealed to each other and to our son and daughter.

Norma Storland passed away in 2012. She was born in Madison, South Dakota, and was the daughter of William August Beyer and Elda Ida Albertina Holler Beyer. As a teenager Norma moved to Minneapolis where she met her husband. They purchased land near Eagan, Minnesota, in what was then sparsely settled countryside, and lived in primitive conditions until her husband could build a proper home. They joined the church in 1980 and later served a mission. She was known for her hard work and her generosity. All who knew her remember her with fondness.

Receiving Answers
to Prayer

The Cell Phone

BY JACKIE KELLINGTON

WE WERE A BIT PUMPED about our first cell phone. It meant we would be able to reach each other without being near a landline phone. For several reasons Chuck and I agreed it was probably best we not share the cell with our children, at least not for a while.

It had been an unusually long day and Chuck returned home from work exhausted. The bed must have been singing some sort of lullaby to him because he retired at a crazy early hour and was zoned out before his head hit the pillow—well, maybe as soon as it hit the pillow.

Rachel, then 17, responded positively to my request to deliver clothing and other items we had accumulated to Goodwill. A close friend offered her help. Of course Rachel knew about the cell phone we had recently purchased. She asked to use it. I paused in my response—that was a mistake. Mind you, I paused only briefly, but it was a mistake nonetheless. I replied, "Not a good idea."

However, Rachel had picked up on my hesitancy. She proceeded to plead with me, expressing several reasons why it made sense for her to use the cell. The reasons were logical. They did make sense. And what if I *did* need to reach her, or what if there was some sort of an emergency and she didn't have access to a phone? That made sense, didn't it? Well, you may have guessed—I let her take my cell.

I, too, was pretty tired and decided to call it a day. The snoring was huge evidence that Chuck was pretty zoned out, but oh, that's right. I forgot. He doesn't snore. (I know because he told me so.)

I don't know what time it was when I fell asleep. I clearly remember being awakened when Rachel opened our bedroom door. Quietly approaching my side of the bed, she whispered, with what sounded like anguish in her voice, that she had lost the cell! If what she was feeling was not anguish, I certainly was. That, and a few other fearful emotions. How ever was I going to tell Chuck? I decided I wasn't—we, Rachel and I, were going to backtrack all of her steps and find the phone. We had to!

I was very careful not to awaken Chuck as I slipped out of bed and quickly dressed. We drove to every place she had been. We particularly searched the area of Goodwill with no luck. It was not just the loss of the cell, but a trust issue. I dreaded daybreak.

Driving back home, Rachel asked me to pray about it. She was convinced if I did we would find the phone. I explained to her that it was she that had lost it and Heavenly Father would respond to her as well as me. But she was not confident in her relationship with the Lord and expressed faith in mine. That brought about mixed feelings, grateful for her faith in prayer, but sadness because she didn't feel she could approach her Heavenly Father herself.

Arriving home, I sought a quiet and private place. My petition was this: I first explained our dilemma and then expressed gratitude for the many times He had responded to my prayers. I was grateful for Rachel's faith in prayer and asked Him to respond, not to me, but rather to Rachel, telling *her* where the lost cell was. I knew that He knew Rachel was not active in Church, but I believed He would respond to her faith.

I hadn't yet gone to sleep again when Rachel quietly came into my room and told me she had found the cell. I felt so relieved and amazed. I asked where she had found it. She responded it was out on the road next to the mailbox. Surprised, I asked her why she thought to look there. She replied, "I don't know, Mom. Something just told me that I would find it there. It was like somebody talking to me."

I am grateful to have shared this experience with Rachel. I believe the memory of it will remain with her always, increasing her faith further.

P.S. I have yet to share the story of the cell phone with Chuck, but I imagine it will soon come to light.

Jacquelyn A. Kellington has a gift for meeting people and learning how special they are. She was born in Minneapolis, Minnesota, and joined the Church in 1963. She has served in many callings, including being a stake missionary and a temple ordinance worker. She is a trained dental surgery assistant and recognizes God's hand in directing her to this profession. She also worked as a certified foster care provider for hard-to-place children and as a nanny for many years. She developed a deep love for the children she cared for. Jackie and her husband, Chuck, have six children of their own. Her parents are John Russel and Hannah Morehead Hoffman.

That all the people of the earth might know the hand of the Lord, that it is mighty: that ye might fear the Lord your God for ever.
Joshua 4:24

The Joy My Children Give Me

BY ABBY VILLANUEVA

ONE NIGHT I CAME HOME very tired from work. I could not make dinner. I requested Shekinah to buy some pizza for dinner. She did and unconsciously put her wallet on the roof of her car before she put the pizza boxes in the car. Then she drove home. As she parked on our driveway, she started to search for her wallet. She panicked. It was gone.

She didn't let me know right away what happened. She tried to fix the problem herself. She went back to the pizza parlor and tried searching where her wallet must have flown off along the way back from the pizza parlor. She was very frustrated. It was gone.

She called me. She was crying and at first I couldn't understand what she was trying to say. It took me a while to understand her. She was very afraid, not only for losing her IDs, especially her green card [permanent resident card], but most of all, she didn't want us, her parents, to scold her for this mistake. She has been told to take care of these important things many, many times. I felt she needed my help more than scolding or blaming or anything like that. I asked her over the phone to calm down and pray for help that we might find her wallet. I would contact the banks to hold her cards. But I told her I had to let her dad know. I needed his advice of what else to do.

Her dad was freaking out about what had happened. As I was explaining to him that Shekinah was very sorry and still out there looking for it, my other children caught my attention. They were in a circle, praying. They were praying for their sister, that someone may return the wallet to us, or that their sister may find it so their dad wouldn't be upset about the situation. My tears rolled down my cheeks. It was one of the greatest moments I've seen with my own eyes—that my children resorted to prayer in unity at this time of need. I knew that we'd be able to find her wallet. I felt comforted and was calmed.

My husband advised me to file a police report. So Shekinah and I went to do so. (That's the first time I've done that in forty-two years!) I felt so awkward and ignorant but wasn't scared at all. It was a late, cold winter night, waiting outside the police station in Rosemount. Speaking over the phone box, I was able to relay what happened. We kept standing outside while the policewoman on the other side of the phone was radioing to the other policemen in the area. About ten minutes later, we were told that someone was on his way to where we were with a story of the whereabouts of the wallet. Soon a policewoman came saying that someone picked up the wallet and gave it to the Cub Foods customer service. Then Cub Foods called a policeman to return the wallet to the owner.

Our family attended General Conference in Salt Lake City for the first time in October 2011. My children are (left to right) Jannica, Hyrum, Shekinah, and Brigham.

That policeman was on his way to meet us. We hugged each other and waited in the car for another fifteen or twenty minutes.

The policeman came apologizing to us for the wait, as he was looking for our house first, when he got the call that we were in the police station. He gave us Shekinah's wallet with everything intact in it.

I know that prayers are answered all the time. I felt so blessed seeing my children being united in prayer and faith.

Abegail "Abby" Villanueva was born in Quezon City, Philippines, and her parents, Peregrino and Marcela Pascual, were members of the Church when she was born. She has a B.S. in chemical engineering and works full-time as a statistical process control manager for a semiconductor company. She and her husband, Elmer, and their four children moved to Apple Valley, Minnesota, from the Philippines in 2007. She loves cooking for her family and being around little children. Their sweet spirits strengthen her and always make her smile.

*Nevertheless, all flesh is in mine hand,
and he that is faithful among you shall not perish ...
Doctrine & Covenants 61:6*

Prayer

by Heather J. Graham

PRAYER IS SOMETHING that does not come easily for me. Or maybe a better way to put it is that receiving answers to prayers doesn't come easily to me.

I'm a person who doesn't tend to have big spiritual experiences. I don't think it's because I'm not open to them. I just think the Lord answers me in other ways.

I do great at the actual praying. Especially during hard times in my life, I've tried even more diligently to pray in specific ways such as increasing the number of my prayers during the day or making sure my prayers are full of the things I'm thankful for. I have tried to go through the day with a prayer always in my heart, and I have tried to wait and just listen after I am finished praying. I have even tried to make my prayers be full of others' needs and not my own, even when my own needs seem to overwhelm my thoughts. But many times I still struggle to feel like I'm receiving answers.

Over the years I have learned a few things about how the Lord's Spirit talks to my spirit. Many times I need to decide on a course or make a decision first. That is what happened when my husband asked me to marry him. I tried to make the Lord decide for me if I should marry him or not. That didn't work out well. I got absolutely no answer. Nothing. Blank. So eventually I told Darren no. But it really bugged me that the Lord hadn't answered this prayer. I mean, who you marry affects so much of your life and your children's lives. So even after we broke things off, I still pondered and thought about his marriage proposal. When I went home for Christmas break, two other boys asked me to marry them. I looked at these boys that I had known in high school. They were good boys, but they weren't the kind of man I wanted to marry. When I changed my prayer from "Should I marry Darren?" to "I want to marry him. Is that the right thing?" that made all the difference and I received my answer. I had decided on a course of action and the Lord could answer me. So when I saw Darren again a few weeks later, I asked him to marry me!

Another thing I have learned to do is wait for the peaceful feeling the Spirit can give you. Many times when I am pondering on a decision, I can get really agitated and frustrated. I want the answer to be clear and easily understood on what to do and usually I want the answer right now. I have learned to wait until I get the peaceful calm feeling from the Lord before making a decision.

The peaceful feeling is hard for me to describe. It's not the same as a lack of agitation or frustration. It's warm, comforting, happy, and relaxing. It's like being in a patch of sunshine with a soft breeze around you and a feeling of warmth through your whole body that you get from being in the sun. When I can feel that peaceful feeling, then the answer that I'm looking for comes.

I know many others receive answers in different ways. I've often wondered what it was like for Nephi to receive answers. He would hear the voice of the Lord, and he would have angels answer his prayers. In 1 Nephi 17 he is commanded to build a ship and the Lord says he will show him the manner in which to build the ship and where to find ore. Did Nephi have images come to his mind of where to go and what to build? I would love to be so in tune to the Spirit that I could receive answers that way!

For now I keep trying to be diligent. I realize the Lord speaks to me through my feelings. He speaks to me when it's quiet or when I'm truly willing to listen to the answer. Sometimes my answers will come when I'm not thinking of them. This usually happens when I'm serving others. I think when I'm serving others, then I'm more in tune to the Spirit.

I'm just grateful that He's patient with me. I truly do feel like receiving personal revelation is a challenge for me. This is probably my lifelong challenge that the Lord and I will work on together. But when I do receive an answer, I try very hard to follow through on the answer so that hopefully with each experience I will become more like Nephi.

Heather J. Graham attended BYU-Provo with a major in speech pathology. She is also fluent in American Sign Language and is often asked to interpret for the hearing impaired at sacrament meetings and stake conference. She has been a stay-at-home mom for eighteen years.

Heather was born in Provo, Utah, the daughter of Brent Whiting and Lynne Ann Richards. She and Darren moved to Minnesota with their six children in 2007.

*Thou has beset me behind and before and laid thine hand upon me...
If I take the wings of the morning and dwell
in the uttermost parts of the sea, even there shall thy hand lead me,
thy right hand shall hold me.
Psalm 139:5, 9–10*

He Hears
My Prayers

BY MEGAN STOTTS

WHEN I PONDER on how I've seen the hand of the Lord in my life, so many experiences come to mind. One of them occurred when I was at a pretty low point in my life. I was trying to do everything the Lord required of me, but I just couldn't do it right. I was feeling very alone and discouraged, so I decided to pray. Through my tears I pleaded with the Lord to let me know that He was there, that He knew me and was aware of my struggles. When I was done praying, I turned to my scriptures. I'd learned over the years that the Spirit impresses upon me most clearly when I read the scriptures. I opened to Doctrine and Covenants 38:7, and this is what I read:

But behold, verily, verily, I say unto you that mine eyes are upon you. I am in your midst and ye cannot see me.

The overwhelming feeling of love that I received was magnificent. I *knew* that Heavenly Father knew who I was, that He was aware of my struggles, and He was always watching over me.

THE HAND OF THE LORD

Another experience when my prayers were answered was at school in my A.P. [Advanced Placement] United States history class. We were preparing for a project on all the state capitals, and my teacher asked for a volunteer to help him with something. Nobody raised a hand, so I decided to help. My task was to write the names of every capital on individual pieces of paper and put them in a hat for the students to draw from. I knew that Salt Lake City would go into the hat, and I was afraid that someone would draw it and could potentially come across false information about the history of the city and the people who live there. As I was writing each city on pieces of paper, I was silently praying that somehow I could be the one to draw it. I knew that Heavenly Father could answer my prayer, and as the hat got passed around, I didn't stop pleading. Salt Lake still hadn't been drawn by the time the hat got to me. I knew this was the moment of truth, the time to see if my faith paid off. I was ready to reach in and pull out Salt Lake City, when my teacher stopped me and said that I could go ahead and choose whichever capital I wanted since I had volunteered to help him. A huge smile appeared on my face as warmth spread through my entire body. Without hesitation I practically shouted, "Salt Lake City!" I was ecstatic. My prayer had been answered so obviously that I could not doubt again. Because my prayer was answered I was able to explain the history of the city and the history of the people as it truly happened, and I was even able to talk about the Church.

I'm grateful for the hand of the Lord in my life, and I know that He will always answer my prayers, and that He *does* know me and *does* watch over me.

Megan Stotts is a senior at Apple Valley High School. She has been active in choir, theater, and orchestra. She plans to attend BYU-Provo where she will study music and Spanish. She was born in Houston, Texas, the daughter of Kelly and Maria Stotts, and moved to Oregon at age 1, the Netherlands at age 10, and Minnesota at age 12. She loves singing and playing the violin.

And when ye see this, your heart shall rejoice...
and the hand of the Lord shall be known toward his servants.
Isaiah 66:14

The Holy Ghost

BY AINSLEY DAVIS

O NE NIGHT when I was about 5 or 6 years old, I was scared of the dark. My mom came in and we said a prayer together to help me not be afraid of the dark. After a few minutes I started to cry because I knew that I was feeling the Holy Ghost comforting me. After that I was not scared any more, so I was able to fall asleep.

I know that the Holy Ghost can always comfort me in times of need.

Ainsley Davis currently attends Scott Highlands Middle School in Apple Valley. She was born in St. Louis Park, Minnesota, and is the daughter of Barton G. and Loni E. Davis. She has two sisters. She enjoys singing, music, acting, and swimming.

The Lost Folder

BY HOLLY THATCHER

I HAD ABOUT A HUNDRED IDEAS of different stories to share for this book. Because I read everyone else's story before this book was published, I would get a new idea just about every day. Almost every story would remind me of a similar experience in my own life. I wrote bits and pieces of several experiences, but I had a hard time sitting down to finish just one. One of the stories I wrote was already several pages long and that was just the backstory to the real story! Clearly I needed help. I'm terrible at making decisions. With just a few hours until the absolute final deadline, I asked my husband his opinion and without hesitation, he suggested, "the lost folder." He thought that was the story I should write because it happened the first week we moved to Minnesota. I thought that might be boring because many people have already heard this experience. I have shared it before in sacrament meeting and in a lesson to the Laurels. But I have never written it down, so that seemed like something I should do.

(Before I start, I feel like I need a little disclaimer here. I'm telling the story the way I remember it and I apologize in advance to those mentioned in the story who may remember it a little differently.)

When we moved to Minnesota, I flew from Salt Lake City with our kids, and Dan drove our car. Our first night all together in Minnesota we stayed in a hotel room that Dan's company paid for. The next morning we went to Edina Realty's Lakeville office to sign the closing papers on our new house. We were all so tired, and it was such a whirlwind week that it was easy to be overwhelmed with all the changes in our life.

After signing our names a million times, we got the keys and a folder of our closing papers and we were on our way. We coordinated with the movers so they would be delivering our stuff right away. I was anxious to see our new house because I had never actually seen it in person. I had only seen it in photos, and Dan was the only one who had walked through it before we made our offer. Just a few minutes after we got to our house, the moving van pulled up. There was a flurry of activity with movers going in and out. I was trying to keep our children, who were then 2 and 6 years old, out of the way.

As our furniture and boxes were pilling up inside, I had a feeling I should make sure I had the folder from our closing in a safe place. I was worried it would get buried under everything. I started looking around the house, but no folder. I asked Dan. He hadn't seen it. Then I asked Emma and Caleb. I asked the movers. No one had seen the folder. I looked in the car. I called Edina Realty's office and had them look to see if we had left it there by mistake. No folder.

I started thinking about everything that was in the folder. It was an identity thief's dream come true. It had copies of our driver's licenses, Social Security cards, credit reports, all of our bank and credit card account numbers, our tax returns, pay stubs, and checks for the amount we made from the sale of our house in Utah, which was more money than we'd ever had at one time. I felt sick.

When the movers had unloaded the last box, Dan decided he should take the kids out to get some lunch. I was too worried about the folder, so I stayed home and continued to look. I went into my new unfamiliar bedroom and prayed. It was really more crying than praying. I felt so angry that the folder was missing. I felt scared of what would happen to us if that folder got into the wrong hands. I felt like maybe this was a terrible omen, that we had made a huge mistake in packing up our family and moving to Minnesota. I remember repeating several times in my prayer, "Please, please help us find this folder."

I tried to really concentrate and think about where it could be. I retraced my steps. I went through the day's events in my mind. Then I remembered that when we had walked out of the office, our 2-year-old Caleb had made a run for it and did not want to hold my hand in the parking lot. As we approached our car door, he let go of my hand again. So I would be able to better pick him up to get him in the car, I set the folder on the roof of the car. After we were all buckled in our seat belts, the folder remained there on the roof of the car. And we drove away.

When Dan got home from lunch I told him what I thought had happened to the folder. He quickly got back in the car to drive the route back to the office to look for it on the side of the road. The folder was made of plastic and had a velcro closure, so I was hoping it would stay in one piece. But I visualized the worst case scenario: that on the roof of the car going 50 miles an hour, the papers would be flung free from the folder and scatter in the wind for miles in every direction. Little bits of all our personal information that we would never be able to gather up and put away.

I prayed and prayed some more. We prayed individually and we prayed as a family. The kids obviously could not understand why mom was so upset about some boring old papers. Because of the drama of the lost folder, we didn't get much of anything unpacked that day. We decided because Dan's company would pay for another night of a hotel room, we would drive back to the Radisson.

As we were getting teeth brushed and pj's on, I got a call from our real estate agent, Kris. Because her business card was in the folder, she had received a message that someone had found our folder and turned it into the police. I had a hard time finishing the conversation because I was so overcome with emotion. We said a prayer of gratitude and then we could finally relax and sleep.

The next morning, we headed to the Apple Valley police station as soon as we could. There was our folder and absolutely everything was still in it. We didn't know who found it and turned it in, so we didn't have anyone to thank except Heavenly Father.

Now this is the part where I can't remember if it was later that day, or the next day, but there was a knock at the door. Two kind-looking people about the age of our parents were at the door. They also appeared to have a plate of treats. I thought they looked safe enough to answer the door for. They introduced themselves as Reo and Merle Pratt and said, "Welcome to the ward!" I was so

This is our son, Caleb, standing in front of our Apple Valley home shortly after we moved here in 2008

surprised that anyone from the ward already knew who we were and where we lived. I invited them inside. Then Merle said, "We found your folder." Hearing those words, I felt enveloped in the warmth of the Spirit and for a second I felt like I couldn't breathe. I was in shock that members of our new ward had found our folder! I felt tears welling up in my eyes, but I tried to hold them back in front of the Pratts.

They told the story of how their daughter Nancy saw the folder leaning up against a tree and picked it up and brought it inside to see what it was. They had tried coming over to our house to return the folder, but we weren't home because we were already back at the hotel. After looking through the contents of the folder, they assumed that we were LDS because they had heard a family was moving from Salt Lake City to the Apple Valley ward. They decided it was best to turn it into the police. I was so happy to have someone to thank for finding our folder. My only disappointment was Dan wasn't home to meet the Pratts and hear their story straight from them.

When I told Dan about what had happened, we talked about where the Pratts live in relation to where we live. Their house is only about a mile away from us, but it's not the street that we would normally drive on to get from County Rd. 42 to our street. Dan remembered how that day he wanted to find our house without using the GPS and he may not have taken the most direct route. Even if we did drive directly past the Pratt's house on the way home, that meant that the folder stayed on the roof of our car for over four miles driving from Lakeville through Apple Valley and fell off at just the right time. To me that fits the definition of a miracle.

Some people might read this story and think that the Pratt family finding our folder is nothing more than a nice coincidence. But as I prayed and pondered the significance this experience had in my life, it was much greater than a nice coincidence. It was a direct and personal answer to prayer. I felt like it was the best way Heavenly Father could calm my anxiety about moving to Minnesota. Through this experience, He showed me that He knows me and my family in a very real way. He loves us. He listens to us. He helps us. I'm grateful for the lost folder. I'm also grateful for this opportunity to reflect back to five years ago and be reminded of the feelings I had and the lessons I learned.

This quotation from President Hinckley sums it up for me:
Things work out, it isn't as bad as you sometimes think it is. It all works out, don't worry. I say that to myself every morn-

ing. It will all work out. If you do your best, it will all work out. Put your trust in God, and move forward with faith and confidence in the future. The Lord will not forsake us. If we will put our trust in Him, if we will pray to Him, if we will live worthy of His blessings, He will hear our prayers.

Holly Thatcher was born in San Francisco, California, to Joy Hurlburt and Don Nelson. She grew up in Concord, California, with one younger sister, Jennifer. Holly graduated from BYU-Provo with a B.A. in English. Two weeks after graduating, she entered the Missionary Training Center and served a mission in the China Hong Kong Mission. Soon after returning home to California, she met her future husband, Dan, at the Berkeley Young Single Adults Ward. They were married on March 18, 2000, in the Oakland Temple. They have lived in Berkeley and Salt Lake City, and they currently make their home in Apple Valley, Minnesota, where they have lived since April 2008. Holly and Dan are the parents of two children, Emma and Caleb.

Alice, the Snake

BY EMILY TENNANT

OUR FAMILY LOVES PETS. We have had several different pets, anything from cats, dogs, tree frogs, fish, birds, hamsters, and guinea pigs. My mom always said she was open to different pets, but was scared to death of snakes. Of course, my dad always loved having pet snakes. One night my dad came home with a surprise, a pet corn snake named "Alice." My mom thought it was okay as long as she didn't have to *ever* feed it and it *never* got lost. She always said if Alice got lost, she would move out until the snake was found. She would have random "Is Alice in her cage?" checks. Alice was always in her cage.

Then one afternoon I invited my friend Lauren over to my house. We decided to play with the snake. My mom said it was okay, so we took Alice up to the crawl space, a storage area in our basement. We had a container with no top, which acted as a cage for the snake in the crawl space, but we were watching her so we knew if she tried to escape. After a little bit we heard my mom call

Emily Tennant: "Alice, the Snake   75

us upstairs for lunch. Being third graders, we didn't think twice about leaving Alice in the container when we went upstairs to eat. My mom made grilled cheese sandwiches and fruit on the side. When Lauren and I were almost finished, she leaned over to me and spelled in a quiet voice, but still urgent, "S-n-a-k-e." At first I didn't understand, but after she finally just said, "The snake!" I realized that we had left Alice in the crawl space in a container with no lid.

We quickly dismissed ourselves from lunch and ran downstairs. We bolted into the crawl space and went over to the container. When we looked inside, there was nothing there, only empty space.

"Oh, no! Now we have to tell my mom, Lauren!" I was freaking out.

"Well, come on. Alice has to still be in here, right?" Lauren replied, just as scared. I nodded my head and we slowly climbed out, not wanting to have to face my mom. We shakily made our way up the stairs.

"Mom?" I called out.

"Over here!" We heard her yell from the kitchen.

"Ummm, we have something to tell you…" I trailed off, not wanting to have to tell her. It was her only rule, not to lose the snake.

"What is it?" she questioned. I looked over to Lauren for support, but she looked as scared as I felt.

"Well…WekindoflostAliceinthecrawlspace," I rushed out.

"What? You were talking way too fast for me to catch what you said." By now we could tell she was getting worried. I took a deep breath and started again, this time slower.

Emily and her younger brother, Andrew, had fun playing with their pet corn snake, Alice.

"We lost Alice in the crawl space." We watched my mom's eyes widen in surprise. She was not expecting that.

"You lost Alice?" I nodded my head slowly.

"Well, we better go find her."

By this time both Lauren and I were crying. "Mommy, you won't move out, will you?" I questioned. I always knew she was joking of course, but I was still worried.

"Of course not, but we better find that snake!" We all headed downstairs to the crawl space. My mom started taking out the storage boxes, one by one, looking for a sign that the snake was there, but we could not find her anywhere!

My mom was growing terrified and overwhelmed by the fact that the snake could be *anywhere*. Of course, my dad was out of town, so my mom had to deal with the lost snake herself. (She did call him in Oregon, but he refused to come home and find the snake.) My mom was convinced that we would never find Alice. I think she was seriously trying to figure out how long it would take her to pack her bags and move in with our neighbor Becky.

Alice was gone for what felt like hours, my mom panicking all the while. Finally, I said, "Mom, we should say a prayer." So we sat down and prayed.

"We left our toys in the back of the crawl space, Mom," I remembered.

"Well, we'll get them later, okay?"

"Nah, Me and Lauren can go get them now, right, Lauren?" We crawled to the back of the crawl space. My mom timidly followed. As we started gathering our toys, Lauren screamed.

"Emily, look!" Lauren pointed over near some old lumber. "It's Alice!" We saw the swish of her tail. Just as the last of Alice's tail was disappearing under the boards, my mom quickly grabbed it. She held on tight as we uncovered the sneaky snake. Soon Alice was back safely locked in her cage.

I am grateful that we said a prayer and I am amazed at how fast that prayer was answered. Even small things are important to the Lord. I am also glad my mom did not have to move out that night.

Emily Tennant was born in Orem, Utah, and moved to Minnesota when she was 6 weeks old. She and her family moved to Apple Valley in 2003. Her parents are Erik and Cathy Tennant and she has two brothers. In the fall Emily will enter eighth grade at Falcon Ridge Middle School. She plays the flute, sings, and has appeared in school musicals. She has danced since she was 4 years old and recently won a dance competition for a dance duet that she and her friend choreographed. She is also a "Directioner" (a fan of the band One Direction). She hopes to go to BYU-Provo five years from now.

And the hand of the Lord was there upon me; and he said unto me, Arise, go forth into the plain, and I will there talk with thee.
Ezekiel 3:22

The Power of Prayer

BY LUCY EKANEM

I HAVE SEEN THE HAND OF GOD in providing a roof over my head. In 2003 my last-born children graduated from high school and were heading to college. I wanted to refinance my home so I could afford to support them with my meager income. That plan failed because of the divorce process. It was a bitter experience to find out at the last minute on April 18, 2003, when the paperwork was ready to be signed but was turned down because my ex-husband refused to sign the documents and demanded I should sell the house. It was a seller's market that year for home owners. My home was sold overnight because of expensive renovations I had made. On the other hand, it was a scary feeling because I would become a buyer now. How would I afford a home with a lean income? If the bank approved at all, then at what interest rate? These were questions in my mind.

One day in May of 2003 my realtor called me at my work and said, "Lucy, I have bad news and good news for you. I will start with the bad news. The house you found in Eagan was sold. The good news is you have been approved for a loan." My heart rate dropped almost automatically because God had taken charge of my need and I would have a roof over my head. My realtor sent fourteen house listings in the email for me to look through before we made a trip to the different locations.

I took half a day off from work that Friday and made a trip to the temple. I stayed in the celestial room praying to God for a shelter for me and my children. It was still bright when I came back from the temple, and I took the list to select the locations I was familiar with to go on my own without waiting for my realtor's schedule on Saturday. As I turned off of Highway 62 on the exit to Highway 77, I pulled to the side of the road to check the list again. While I did so, I meditated, asking God to lead me to the house He saw as best for me.

I drove straight to a house in Apple Valley with the number 15722. It had almost exactly the same house number as my Minneapolis home which was 5722. The Lord is mindful of our needs. Sometimes our trials could be overwhelming and lead us to a point of despair, but He moves in a very mysterious way to answer our prayers. The house was under the approved loan amount and I obtained a lower interest rate than I anticipated.

When our Savior's mortal journey was drawing to the end, He went to the Garden of Gethsemane to pray, asking the Father for a change of mind for such a heavy burden. Why did the Son of God have to pray, even when He can do and undo? Matthew 25:36-44 gives us the perspective for prayer, the powerful tool we must use for our daily undertakings.

I was young and naïve about spiritual matters, but now I understand why my father, who was a pastor in the Episcopal church, held family prayer meetings mornings and evenings. I see myself praying more than twice a day because my patriarchal blessing cautioned me to be constant in prayer.

I am grateful for this knowledge through my patriarchal blessing. Through prayer, God has unveiled the mystery of tithing for me. I have hope, though the road may seem foggy at times. I have gained personal revelation for comfort in time of distress. Surely, knowledge is power. I testify if you pray, God will help you find the right path for your own journey as He has done for me. He has carved me in the palms of His hands (Isaiah 49:16) through the Atonement and the gospel of His Son. In the name of Jesus Christ, amen.

Lucy Ekanem was born in Calabar, in the state of Cross River, Nigeria. In 1978 she moved to Utah to pursue an education. She graduated from the University of Utah and then in 1984 she moved to Minnesota to obtain a graduate degree in business finance from the University of Minnesota. She was baptized in 1988 and later received her endowments in the Chicago Temple, being sealed to her parents, Nkoyo Inyang and Essien Ekanem, on the same day. She has five children and one grandchild. Lucy has a passion for volunteerism, reading, and traveling to see natural wonders such as Old Faithful in Wyoming. She also enjoys visiting Church history sites.

Blessed with a Needed Gift

BY GINGER HAMER

I AM A PERSON who does not recognize faces well. I am so bad with face recognition that, when I'm watching a movie and the scene changes, I often have to ask my husband if these are the same characters we had seen before. I can't seem to keep them straight in a new setting and different clothes.

I was rather new in the ward when I was called to serve as Relief Society president. Although I had tried to get acquainted with people, I still had trouble with names and faces.

Four days after being set apart I attended Recipe Night at the home of one of the sisters. I felt nervous and unsure of myself. Several women were there ahead of me—some of whom I actually recognized. When I came in, they suggested that we get started. But I looked around and said that I thought Tonia, my secretary, was going to come and maybe we should wait for her. Someone laughed, pointed to the woman who was sitting right in front of me at the counter and said, "She's right here."

I was mortified. Of course she was there. I couldn't miss her, but I hadn't recognized this woman with whom I had already served for a couple of months in the previous presidency, whom I knew well enough to suggest to the bishop that she continue in her calling, and with whom I had met in a lengthy presidency meeting only three days earlier. Somehow in this new context, she looked like someone I had never seen before.

So I shook my head, as though to clear it, and laughed and said, "Tonia, of course you're here. Well, let's get started." The rest of the evening of cooking demonstrations and shared recipes went well, but inside I was reeling.

I could hardly wait to get home. I sank to my knees beside my bed and through my tears pleaded for the blessing of being able to recognize faces and remember names. I affirmed that I was willing to serve and was grateful for the calling, but I didn't know how I could accomplish His work if I couldn't recognize my own secretary, let alone all the other people in the ward. I was on my knees a long time that night. The Lord heard my prayer.

Now, two years later, I testify that what the prophet has told us is true: whom the Lord calls, He qualifies. The ability I have had for the past two years to recognize faces and remember names is a gift directly from God, and I acknowledge His hand. Along with this gift, He has also blessed my heart with a profound love for the sisters of the Apple Valley Ward. Once again I have been shown that we must not let our inadequacies prevent us from accepting a calling. The Lord will magnify even our inabilities; all we have to do is be willing to serve.

Ginger Hamer was born in Denver, Colorado, but grew up in Aurora, Illinois, where she attended a small branch of the Church that met in the Odd Fellows Hall. She is the oldest child of Robert L. and Louise G. Erekson and has nine younger brothers. She served a mission to Brazil, graduated from BYU-Provo, and taught high school English for two years. Then she was a stay-at-home mom while her five children were young. The family moved to Minnesota in 1980, and she and her husband, Bill, moved to Apple Valley in 2010. Ginger enjoys entering baked goods and hand-quilted baby quilts in the Minnesota State Fair.

Know ye not that ye are in the hands of God?
Know ye not that he hath all power?
Mormon 5:23

A Child's Prayer

BY JACQUELINE A. KELLINGTON

MY DAUGHTER DEBBIE, who lives in Oregon, was making preparations for the evening dinner. Bryan, her second grader, was sitting on the kitchen counter watching, or rather "helping." But he was quiet and appeared pensive, not his usual chatty self. He suddenly asked his mom if he could pray for his dad's safety. Debbie was touched by Bryan's request and responded, "Of course, Bryan, we can do that tonight in our evening prayer." His response was strong, "No, Mom, not tonight, now. We need to do it now!" Concerned and a little startled, but respecting her son's feelings, she set dinner preparations aside to pray with her young son for his father's safety.

Jim traveled the mountains of Oregon frequently for his work. On this particular day and time, he was driving through a mountain pass. To his right, the river seemed higher than usual and particularly turbulent. Coming down this mountain road toward him was a semitruck carrying a large load of huge cement culverts. One of those culverts fell to the road. Bouncing and rolling, it headed straight towards Jim's car. He felt a sense of panic.

85

He could not avoid it by turning to the right, that would put him into the river. If he turned to the left, he would most certainly collide with the semi. The culvert had picked up momentum. Just as it was to hit Jim's car, it suddenly broke that momentum, and directly in front of him, bounced up and over the car and landed in the river.

The driver of the semi stopped on the side of the road. Getting out of the cab, he walked over to Jim and exclaimed, "I thought for sure you were a goner." Jim was also breathless and could hardly believe what he had just experienced.

He drove to the next town, anxious to find a phone to share with his wife what had just happened. As he did so, Debbie shared with him the experience she had with their son Bryan. They calculated together that the prayer for his safety was only minutes before the event, an event that could have ended in a great tragedy. Jim's life was spared because his young son was sensitive to the Spirit. They remain grateful for the power of prayer and for the Lord's intervention in their lives.

Jacquelyn A. Kellington has a gift for meeting people and learning how special they are. She was born in Minneapolis, Minnesota, and joined the Church in 1963. She has served in many callings, including being a stake missionary and a temple ordinance worker. She is a trained dental surgery assistant and recognizes God's hand in directing her to this profession. She also worked as a certified foster care provider for hard to place children and as a nanny for many years. She developed a deep love for the children she cared for. Jackie and her husband, Chuck, have six children of their own. Her parents are John Russel and Hannah Morehead Hoffman.

He Continues to Walk By My Side

BY CATHY TENNANT

WHEN I WAS 12 YEARS OLD, my Young Women's teacher gave each of us a copy of the poem "Footprints." It describes a dream in which a person is walking on a beach with Heavenly Father. They leave two sets of footprints in the sand behind them. Looking back, the person can see that the tracks represent various stages of his life. At some points, however, especially at the lowest and most hopeless moments of the character's life, the two trails dwindle to one. The person asks God, "Why did you abandon me when I needed you most?" God gives the explanation: "During your times of trial and suffering, when you see only one set of footprints, that was when I carried you." As a young Beehive girl, I loved this imagery. I had a naïve notion of what it really meant to be carried by God, and I began to look for times in my life when I had been carried by the Lord.

Although I have not thought about this specific poem in many years, I have not forgotten its message. Looking back on my life, I know that I was carried through scary surgery, a devastating

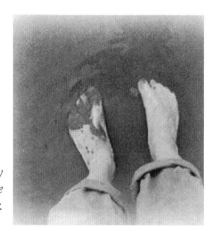

Leaving footprints on the sandy beaches of the Oregon coast where my family vacations each summer.

miscarriage, the loss of family members, and other personal trials. I also know that I will continue to be carried through future difficult events in my life. But the Lord does not only show His hand in my life during times of great need, but also in seemingly insignificant events too. I have been blessed with a clear, calm head during tests, the confidence to walk into a room of strangers, energy to get my work done, and inspiration to teach my children.

Tonight, as I write, I am reminded of one small prayer that was answered in a very special way. As I finished my degree and licensure as a teacher, I began to look for a job. I always thought Erik (and our family) was lucky to have a job with flexible hours. Being in the education field, I knew that I would not be so lucky. A teacher's schedule is pretty much set. I began to worry about how going to work would impact my children's daily lives. I knew that because my children are older, they would be fine if I had to be at work while they were at home for a few hours, but it still troubled me.

I knelt down and said a prayer. I asked Heavenly Father to please help me find a job that would have the least impact on my children's lives. I wasn't sure how the Lord would answer my prayer, but I put my worries in His hands. Not long after I said this prayer, the St. Paul School District offered me a position assessing and teaching children ages birth to 3 who might benefit from early intervention. This job is a direct answer to my prayer. It has proven to be one of the few jobs in the education field where I can have the flexibility that was so important to me (and my children). I am so happy and grateful for the times, like this one, when the Lord has walked side-by-side with me in my life.

Cathy Tennant was born in White Plains, New York, and lived in New Jersey and Ohio before moving with her family to Minnesota in 1980. She is the daughter of Bill and Ginger Hamer. She met her husband, Erik, at BYU. They and their three children moved to Apple Valley in 2003. Cathy holds a B.S. in psychology from BYU and an M.A. from the University of Minnesota in early childhood and early childhood special education. Cathy is easy to talk to and she is a loyal friend. She enjoys reading and photography and would like to find time to bring her much-neglected blog up to date.

The Magically Perfectly Clean House

BY LONI DAVIS

I WOKE UP GRUMPY, ornery, and impatient with how messy the house was. I was frustrated and tired. Ainsley was 6, Kenzie was 4, and Summer was 1½. It was a Saturday morning and Bart had already left for work that day. I was irritated that I worked so hard to keep our house clean, and I felt like no one cared enough to even try and help clean up after themselves. In this irritable mood I said the prayer on the kids' breakfast food. In a fatigued, sarcastic voice I ended the prayer with "And please bless that this house will magically get clean." I realized what a silly request that was to say in a prayer, but my mood spoke it.

While the girls were eating their breakfast, I noticed we were doing quite well on timing before we had to leave for their gymnastics class, so I suddenly had the desire to at least try and empty the dishwasher before we left. I quickly got that done, then thought, wouldn't that be nice to come home to a clean sink? So, while the girls got their socks and shoes on, I not only loaded the dishwasher with the dirty dishes but I handwashed all the big pots, pans, and colanders that were left in the sink. I thought to myself that was pretty cool how quickly I got that done.

Once we got home from gymnastics I started right away on a project I had wanted to do for months—the fridge. I enlisted the girls to do some extra jobs for money after they had done their regular job of putting their clothes away. Ainsley put all the shoes away that had piled up in the front closet and Kenzie Windexed the sliding glass door, the oven door, the windows above the sink and all the shelves in the fridge that I was cleaning. And they did this all with out fussing! The girls ate a snacky lunch so I didn't even have to stop to cook something for them.

I took a quick break to eat my own lunch, then stopped to play Memory and Go Fish with the girls. I got a quick half hour snooze before Summer woke up from her nap. After that, all the girls went out to play with the neighbor kids. While they were out playing, I cleaned the kitchen counters, swept, and mopped the kitchen floor and entryway, and I even cleaned the floor underneath the refrigerator! I thoroughly Pledged down the kitchen table and all six chairs. I got our bed made and wiped down the bathroom. I "magically," if you want to call it that, had the desire *and* the time to do all of that. As an added bonus, I got to listen to General Conference all the while.

I felt great that I had accomplished so much. The house was clean! It looked and felt great. Even though I had said that morning prayer sarcastically and irritably, my Heavenly Father really did bless me that day. The Lord does not answer our prayers magically by doing things for us. But through our own hard work and effort the Lord can answer our prayers and bless us to accomplish many great things.

Loni Davis is a life-long Minnesotan, having been born in St. Paul. She lived for six years in Utah while pursuing a degree in humanities at BYU-Provo. She has been a travel agent and is now a stay-at-home mom and pre-school gymnastics coach. She is also serving as Young Women's president in the Apple Valley Ward. Loni and her husband, Barton, have three daughters. Her parents are Stewart E. Peterson and Sharon A. Palmer.

*The Lord did hear my cries, and did answer my prayers,
and has made me an instrument in his hands...
Mosiah 23:10*

BEING GUIDED
ALONG LIFE'S PATH

The Road Back to a Growing Testimony

BY LYNNETTE HOWZE

I HAVE ALWAYS HAD A TESTIMONY. That was never the question. What I didn't realize is that if I didn't keep it growing by doing and by sharing, it would end up hidden on the back of a shelf somewhere. So over the course of twenty-one years, my testimony found its way on a shelf collecting dust. I had chosen a harder road to travel in life (not on purpose), and the consequences became more than I could handle. It started out slow; I went from going to all my church meetings to going to sacrament meeting on Sunday and then going home. Then I started to miss a Sunday here and there altogether. I stopped going to the church activities and interacting with the sisters in the ward. I'd tell myself I was okay because I had a testimony; I was just "semi-inactive." Then I began to feel inadequate and not worthy of receiving the blessings that the gospel and Church membership brings. All of those blessings were for those better than me. It even got to the point where I stopped praying because I felt I wasn't anyone worth listening to, so why would Heavenly Father?

95

I stopped believing that I was redeemable. I had gotten myself into this mess and felt like I had to get myself out of it alone. I didn't know where to start.

The road back started with simple conversations with someone who I consider a spiritual giant. He taught me how to pray again. He taught me how to pray "real." So I started working on that. It felt strange at first. I wondered how Heavenly Father could listen to me. But as time went by I started to feel different. I started listening and I found myself praying all the time. I knew I needed to do more and that I needed to be in a place where I could do more, but where? The Lord answered that prayer too, sending me nearly 1,000 miles from my two sons and friends, back to Minnesota where I grew up. I went home to Minnesota not knowing what was in store for me. But the Lord knew. He knew I needed reestablishment with long ago church friends. He knew I needed to start building relationships in a new ward. He knew that I needed to realize that, YES, I was someone of importance, YES, I was worth loving and, YES, I was worth saving. He also knew that this new road I was taking was not going to be easy. Going through a divorce is hard enough, but losing my employment too—well, blessings do come in strange packages sometimes! I'm learning to rely on the strength my Heavenly Father gives me. I'm learning to ask for the things I need and to realize that if it's right, it will be granted. I'm learning to do things the Lord's way and not my way. I worked to get my temple recommend renewed and have enjoyed going to the temple quite a bit. In fact, I'm quite drawn to it. I find peace inside those temple walls. I'm finding that I read the scriptures more often. I have started devouring church magazines and church books. There are two sentences in a particular book, *Believing Christ* written by Stephen E. Robinson, that really stood out for me. He said: "Not only must we believe that He is who He says He is, we must also believe that He can do what He says He can do. We must not only believe *in* Christ, we must also *believe Christ* when He says He can clean us up and make us celestial."

Alma 32: 33-37 talks about planting a seed:

And now, behold, because ye have tried the experiment, and planted the seed, and it swelleth and sprouteth, and beginneth to grow, ye must needs know that the seed is good.
And now, behold, is your knowledge perfect? Yea, your knowledge is perfect in that thing, and your faith is dormant; and this because you know, for ye know that the word hath swelled your souls, and ye also know that it hath sprouted up, that your understanding doth begin to be enlightened, and your mind doth begin to expand.
O then, is not this real? I say unto you, Yea, because it is light, and whatsoever is light, is good, because it is discernible, therefore ye must know that it is good; and now behold, after ye have tasted this light is your knowledge perfect?
Behold I say unto you, Nay; neither must ye lay aside your faith, for ye have only exercised your faith to plant the seed that ye might try the experiment to know if the seed was good.
And behold, as the tree beginneth to grow, ye will say: Let us nourish it with great care, that it may get root, that it may grow up, and bring forth fruit unto us. And now behold, if ye nourish it with much care it will get root, and grow up, and bring forth fruit.

What was happening to me? I'll happily tell you. I started believing Christ and was finding my spiritual self again. That person who I used to be so long ago was returning. I have found that seed and replanted it. I water it daily and watch it grow stronger and stronger. I have learned that I can't take for granted that I have a testimony. I have to work at it daily. I do know that I am a daughter of God, that He loves me and wants me to succeed. I have learned that YES, I am someone of importance; YES, I am worth loving; and YES, I am worth saving.

Lynnette Howze was born in Minneapolis and grew up in the Church. She is the daughter of Richard and Barbara Bradford. She served a mission to Houston, Texas, and attended the University of Utah on a flute scholarship. She moved to the Apple Valley Ward in 2009. She currently works in the finance department of the Minneapolis Veterans Affairs Medical Center. She has two sons, one studying at the University of Washington and one serving as a Marine in Afghanistan. Lynnette especially loves scrapbooking, reading, music, and phone calls from her boys.

The Right Place at the Right Time

BY MINDY BARRINGER

WE WERE LIVING IN MICHIGAN in April of 2007 and decided it was time to leave. We were hoping to return home to Utah, but that wasn't in the cards for us. Instead, Jeremy got a transfer, so we packed up and moved to Minnesota. We didn't know much about anything here, but we came for a weekend, looked at houses, and bought one! Everything fell into place and we felt like this was where we should be.

In August of that same year, my mom called to tell me my dad had cancer. It was one of the more manageable of the cancers, but we were all very shaken at hearing the "c" word. We immediately had a family fast as we waited for word on the next step. Doctors in Utah said it would be at least a month or two before he'd be able to have surgery, and the options he was given were all very invasive. At this point, we all just wanted it to be gone, and we knew waiting that long would be torture.

My parents had already planned a trip to come visit us in Minnesota in just a week or so, and they were debating about whether or not to still come. This is when it occurred to me that we lived very close to the Mayo Clinic. We thought it was a long shot, but my parents called and were able to get an appointment near the beginning of their trip. The doctors at the Mayo Clinic were amazing! Not only did my mom and dad feel so much comfort, but they were offered much less invasive options. We didn't think there would be any way in the world that they would be able to have the surgery done while they were here, but the Lord knew what we needed. They were able to extend their trip and have the surgery the following week. Then they spent the next two weeks with us while my dad recovered. We felt so blessed to have them with us and to be able to help them after all they've done for us.

I have no doubt that the Lord's hand was in this experience. It was no coincidence that everything worked out so perfectly for my family. I know that our Father in Heaven knows what we need, when we need it, and I am so grateful for that.

Mindy Barringer was born in Malad, Idaho, and is the daughter of Dennis and Sherrie Evans. Mindy earned a degree in management from Utah State University in 2000. She and her husband, Jeremy, have four children. They moved to Minnesota in 2007. Mindy enjoys crafts, reading, and watching her children learn new things.

The Lord's Plan for Me

BY DeAnna Larson

M Y LIFE HAD GONE ACCORDING TO PLAN—almost. I had served a mission in Venezuela (Spanish-speaking, the obvious course, since I had already studied Spanish in high school and college). But I had never really intended to serve as a missionary; it just became the right thing for me to do as I approached 21. Then I had returned home, fully ready for that next step in my life, marriage and a family. Only, they didn't come. I finished my bachelor's degree at BYU, surrounded by single young adult men, faithful priesthood holders who had served missions and would be good husbands and fathers. But I either liked them or they liked me; it never seemed to be mutual. Why couldn't I find the right person for me? Would I ever?

Then one day I received an invitation, along with my other siblings, to come live at the home place in Texas while my brother, the steward of the house, took a military transfer to another assignment. I considered it for a few seconds and then brushed it aside as not being the right time in my life for such a big change. However, the thought kept coming back to me time and again as others in the family declined the offer. Finally one day I decided to think it over again. Why not? I could go wherever I wanted, as I had no family attachments where I was. But was it the right thing for me to do? I wanted to be in the right place if the right person came along. My options were definitely more plentiful in Utah Valley than in my small hometown in Texas.

So I prayed about it. I asked Heavenly Father what would be the best course for me, stay in Utah or move back to Texas? The answer surprised me: "Follow your heart." I was so focused on doing what the Lord wanted me to do that I had really not even considered what I wanted to do. So I put the question to myself: "Heart, what do you want to do?" Again, the answer surprised me: I wanted to go home to Texas. I prayed about my feelings and felt my answer confirmed. Off to Texas I would go.

In small ways, I felt the Lord being mindful of me as I prepared for my move back home—things like having to buy a washer and dryer and a kitchen table and chairs with a minimal amount of money. Then, when I arrived in Texas, I had only a certain amount of money to get me by until I could find employment. As my money dwindled down and I still had not secured a job, I was starting to get a little anxious. But one day, out of the blue, I got a letter from a dear friend, saying she had been thinking of me and wanted to send along a little something to help tide me over until I could get work. The amount was just what I needed. Right after that, I accepted a job in a neighboring town where I made some very dear friends and had a good work experience.

As I settled into my childhood home, living alone, I felt very content. Here was a deep sense of connection to my roots. My father was buried nearby, and I went to his grave often where I could enjoy the solitude of the sacred cemetery and take time to talk with my Heavenly Father. It was truly a time of peace and enjoyment for me.

But social prospects were still limited. I had just turned 30. It seemed that my social possibilities through church or work were either too young or too old. How was I to meet anyone without driving two hours for a singles dance, just to talk to someone over blaring music? The Spirit nudged me in the direction of the Internet. Hadn't some of my friends tried some online sites to meet other people of our faith? But I couldn't wrap my mind around it. What a crazy way to meet people, especially if you were looking to settle down! Nonetheless, the idea still kept coming to mind, so I gathered up my courage and went online to ldssingles.com. I started to make a personal profile and just couldn't get through it. It was too degrading to post myself "for sale" as it seemed.

But the Spirit kept nudging me, so I tried again—and again. It took me about three times to finally set up a personal profile online. I had to be in just the right mood to write it; by the third attempt I decided to have fun with it so I wouldn't come across as desperate. I determined that what I was really trying to accomplish was make friends, not look for a husband. That way, I could wrap my mind around the idea of being online.

Soon after, I got an email from Flyboy. He was sending out a mass email to new people on the site to introduce himself and invite them to look at his website. I went to his website and found out that he lived in Minnesota. "That's safe!" I thought, as I had been worried about personal safety since I lived alone in the country. I figured that if Flyboy was in a distant state, there wasn't any harm in being friends since he couldn't easily show up on my doorstep unannounced.

I sent an email to Flyboy Fred, thus beginning an exchange of emails that became more and more interesting as we found out more about each other. I was impressed with his love of music as well as his correct punctuation and spelling. As our basic knowledge of each other grew, we became very comfortable "talking" to each other through email.

Then it happened. He pushed my comfort zone just a little bit: "Could I call you sometime?" I wasn't ready for that yet. I was enjoying talking through the security of email. Giving out my phone number was a little scary for me. After debating how to answer his question, I decided to be honest by responding that yes, I would like to talk with him on the phone, but I was hesitant to give out my phone number since I lived alone. He replied by suggesting some options to protect my phone number when initiating a call. I was grateful for his respect for my feelings and decided to go ahead and call him. Our first phone call, we talked for a couple of hours. It was very comfortable, and it was nice to put a voice to the email persona. We started talking once a week by phone, and our conversations got longer and longer until one day, we talked for five hours! Phone calls were a very natural next step. We both felt the hand of the Lord guiding us along.

Then it happened again: "Could I come and visit you?" Whoa. I was not ready for that yet. I was comfortable with our emails and weekly phone calls. I was proceeding very cautiously, but as I thought and prayed about it, I decided to accept the offer. So

DeAnna Dean and Fred Larson, happily engaged, July 3, 2003

it was that I met Fred at the Houston airport on Memorial Day weekend. We had a nice visit, with several events planned with friends and families so we wouldn't be alone. Again, it was a very comfortable next step, putting a face to words and then a voice. We felt it was a natural extension of our growing friendship.

It was sometime in June, not long after the Memorial Day trip, that we were talking on the phone and the subject of marriage came up. We both were interested in pursuing the relationship further and felt very comfortable with each new dimension of the person we were getting to know. We hoped it would lead to marriage but couldn't tell yet. Then my heart blurted out, "I want to marry you, Fred," to which he replied that he wanted to marry me, too. "So does this mean we are unofficially engaged?" he asked, to which I replied, "I guess so!" But we still wanted to pray about it and make sure it was the right thing before committing officially.

In search of a very important answer, I took some time to visit my dad's grave. The cemetery was peaceful and quiet. I had a long, silent prayer with my Heavenly Father as I sat on the cemetery bench. I poured out my heart to Him, telling Him of my desire to marry Fred and asking if it was right. My answer was, "He will take good care of you." I felt such an outpouring of love from my Heavenly Father at that moment that I knew it was the right decision. Remembering it now still brings tears to my eyes.

We were officially engaged on July 3rd, when I came to Minnesota to meet his family. On November 7, 2003, we were sealed in the Houston temple, approximately nine months after Fred's first email to me. I moved to Minnesota immediately after. And that is how I found my sweetheart and was sealed in the temple—not according to my plan, but according to the plan of the Lord, for I felt His hand guiding me from friendship into love. He led us both along swiftly yet gently, and we felt His hand guiding us at each step along the way. I know Heavenly Father is mindful of each of us because we are His beloved sons and daughters.

DeAnna Larson was born in Dallas, Texas. She is the fifth of seven children but the first to be born in the covenant. Her parents, John and Betty Anne Dean, were baptized and sealed before she was born. She has a bachelor's degree in elementary education from BYU-Provo and worked as a third grade teacher. She then became an academic advisor at BYU and later at Sam Houston State University in Texas. She has been a stay-at-home mom for the past nine years. She and her husband, Fred, have four children. With their move to Apple Valley in 2012, they created a music room on the first floor of their home. Playing the piano is one of DeAnna's favorite things, along with reading and cooking. She also likes the colors purple and hot pink.

From Rebellion to Understanding

BY GINGER HAMER

In December 1984 I was already looking forward to the following September when my youngest child would enter kindergarten. I relished the thought of all the time that would be mine to develop a career as a freelance writer. I thought I could help earn money to send our children to college. I had been praying for the Lord's direction in this career choice—of course I was really asking only for His rubber stamp approval of my plans. I had it all figured out. But I thought it was only right to ask for direction, and if possible, for His help in finding a way to teach my family more about serving others. Well, you have to be really careful what you ask for in your prayers because this is what happened as recorded in my journal on December 26, 1984:

"Between Sunday School and the Senior Primary program with Cathy and Ben, Br. Matt Smith, a counselor in the bishopric, really blew my world away. He asked to see me and Bill in the bishop's office and called me to be Young Women's president. I was really stunned, very upset and disappointed. My first reaction was the unfairness of the bishopric—that they should have the

right to reach into someone's life, just when I was getting everything in order and under control, and cause complete upheaval,
that they should demand the time involvement and emotional
commitment without regard to where I was in my life. I was just
on the verge of being able to handle everything and reach out and
begin work as a publicist or freelance writer. With my beautiful new office, my computer, my typewriter, I was developing a
self-image of a successful businesswoman and entrepreneur. I had
plans to begin making this image a reality immediately after the
holidays. But first I wanted to take care of Christmas for my family without any outside pressures.

"I was also stunned by the time involvement of a YW
president. You have to go to dances and firesides and overnights
and all of the millions of youth activities and you have to have fun
at them and appreciate silly, mindless teenagers. I don't know how
to have fun and I don't know how to banter, etc. etc. etc.

"Well, I was so upset that though I tried to stay at church,
I couldn't. I drove home even knowing I could stay only ten minutes and then I would have to go back and get everyone.

"Full of tears of resentment and sorrow and twenty-five
other emotions, I headed into my study. I thought, 'Now wouldn't
it be nice if I could open my scriptures and find a passage to answer my problems?' And in the same breath I thought, 'I can't do
that, so full of anger and lack of faith as I am now.' So I just knelt
and prayed desperately, sorry to feel such rebellion in my heart,
but still feeling it very very real. Finally I did need some comfort
so I tried to find a scripture I knew of and turned to a passage I
had previously marked in Psalm 37. (That is, I didn't mean to turn
to it, I was looking for another passage, but this one came up.) It

says: 'Trust in the Lord and do good; so shalt thou dwell in the land, and verily thou shalt be fed. Delight also thyself in the Lord; and he shall give thee the desires of thine heart...' What can I say?"

So I went back to church and picked up my family. Even though I was still numb and emotionally unsettled, I knew the calling was right for me. In spite of my rebellion, with one magnificent passage, the Lord had answered my concerns about accepting the calling ("Trust in the Lord and do good"), paying for college ("verily thou shalt be fed") and having a career ("he shall give thee the desires of thine heart"). I accepted the calling, and the Lord wrought a change in my heart. I learned to love the magnificent teenagers of our ward and serve them gladly.

Fast-forward several years. My husband, a convert of thirty years, decided for reasons of his own to leave the Church. I was devastated. This was not the outcome I had expected from a temple marriage. I felt betrayed, and most of all, I felt angry. Coming to this course of action took my husband almost ten years, and so it would be impossible for me to detail the emotional turmoil of those years and the countless answers to prayers that I received during that time (and since). One occasion is pertinent here.

Looking for comfort one day, I again turned to the scriptures, and I remembered that Psalm 37 had helped me in the past. This time I began reading at verse 7:

Rest in the Lord, and wait patiently for him; fret not thyself because of him who prospereth in his way, because of the man who bringeth wicked devices to pass.
Cease from anger, and forsake wrath; fret not thyself in any wise to do evil.

> For evildoers shall be cut off; but those that wait upon the Lord, they shall inherit the earth.

Once again the Lord spoke to me through this psalm. With these words He reminded me He was still in charge, He knew what was going on, and I was the one who needed to learn an essential lesson. I would not be held responsible for my husband's choices—I could not control what he did—but I *would* be held responsible for my own reactions. I could choose to continue as an "evildoer" or I could "cease from anger" and "rest in the Lord."

Through this experience I learned that in the final judgment we stand as individuals before the Lord. This is a comforting doctrine. It doesn't matter what anyone else does. It doesn't matter what your husband does or what your kids do. Their good choices won't get you into the celestial kingdom, and their less desirable choices won't keep you out. Do you help them and love them and serve them no matter what they choose? Yes! Are you responsible for their choices? No! You are only responsible for what you can control. In the end it doesn't matter if you are married or not, if you have children or not, if you have a career or are a stay-at-home mom. It doesn't matter if you are rich or poor, healthy or plagued by chronic illness. Nothing matters except your own actions given your circumstances, your own faith and obedience, and the choices that you make. And through it all, the Lord is infinitely caring. He stands ready to bless, and He wants all of us to return to Him.

Ginger Hamer was born in Denver, Colorado, but grew up in Aurora, Illinois. She is the oldest child of Robert L. and Louise G. Erekson and has nine younger brothers. She served a mission to Brazil, graduated from BYU-Provo, and taught high school English for two years. Then she was a stay-at-home mom while her five children were young. The family moved to Minnesota in 1980. Ginger obtained a master's degree from the University of Minnesota and worked for fourteen years as a writer and museum exhibit developer. She and her husband Bill moved to Apple Valley in 2010.

O Lord God, thou hast begun to shew thy servant thy greatness, and thy mighty hand; for what god is there in heaven or in earth, that can do according to thy works and according to thy might?
Deuteronomy 3:24

Heavenly Father Found Me

BY POLLY J. PARSONS

THIS SWEET BOOK is not the place to share my deepest wounds, but suffice it to say, when my first marriage ended, I felt lost and pointless. I gave away all that I cared about and moved away from all who knew me so I could end my life. Those were dark days. I was so angry inside—angry at my parents, at my ex-husband, at myself, and at God. I hid myself from all who loved me. I didn't tell anyone where I was going. I just disappeared. I didn't believe I was worth anything and I thought whether I lived or died wouldn't matter to anyone, not even to my children. I moved several states away and began living with a friend's family. I entered into a relationship and ended up pregnant. (Here God's hand was reaching out to me. He knew I would never end my life when I was carrying a child because I loved children so much.) I made friends with a Baptist preacher who spent many hours counseling me, which began the healing process.

One night, around nine o'clock, the matron of the family called me from upstairs to the living room. I was shocked to find the missionaries standing in the middle of the living room. They told me they were late getting back to their apartment, but as they drove by the house, the Spirit was so strong and guided them to knock on the door. They visited with me for a few minutes and set up an appointment to come back. When we visited next, I broke down and told them everything about my life, how I came to be living with this family, and that I was pregnant and not married. The missionaries talked me into meeting with the bishop. I don't remember much about the counsel I received, except I realized that I needed to go home. My dad and I had had a strained relationship for the previous ten years, but I called him and told him I needed to come home. He welcomed me and encouraged me to be strong and to make the trip home.

I learned how much my Heavenly Father and my earthly father love me. Both helped me go home and, along with my bishop in my hometown, helped me set my life right. More time went by before I could realize even a small particle of how much Jesus Christ loves me, but sending the missionaries to me that night was the beginning of my long journey back from the darkness, back into His presence, and back into full fellowship in the Church. I bear my testimony that Christ knows us individually and is concerned for our well-being. His love is bigger than any of our problems if we will just let Him work in our lives.

Polly J. Parsons is a doctoral student in education leadership with a master's degree as a reading specialist. She loves biographies, audio books, campfires, and movies and popcorn. Born in Oklahoma City, Oklahoma, the daughter of Frank and Delpha Rosson, P.J. is a convert to the Church and was baptized in Fort Smith, Arkansas in 1977. She and her husband, Michael, moved to Minnesota in 2012. They have a blended family of six children.

I went in bitterness, in the heat of my spirit;
but the hand of the Lord was strong upon me.
Ezekiel 3:14

Where He Needs Us to Be

BY NIKHOM BAILEY

I LEFT HOME FOR THE MARINE CORPS in the spring of 1993. I was converted into the Church in May of 2006.

I continued living away from my family for all those years until the spring of 2011. We would visit my family in Minnesota yearly for two weeks at a time, and that visit was plenty of time spent with my side of the family. But driving away from my childhood home always made me sad, and tears would well up. My sweet parents were getting old and I felt bad leaving them. But we had a wonderful life in Utah, surrounded by my husband's family, great friends, and a wonderful ward. What more could I ask for?

In May 2011 I told my husband that I was ready to go home. I had mentioned in the past about moving, but it was never anything serious. He knew at that moment that I was serious. We talked about his job and selling our home. We both knew that if Heavenly Father needed us in Minnesota that He will guide us and help us.

Fast forward to September. A family made an offer on our home that we accepted. My husband's job hunt was a waiting game. Our house was sold, but we weren't sure if we were moving across the country or moving into an apartment. We were waiting to hear from his company about a job transfer to Minnesota. A week before closing, the offer letter came and all our prayers were answered. We rented a moving truck, flew my brother out to help drive, and closed on our home the very same day we left the state.

I know that without prayer and faith in our Heavenly Father, this move and relocation would not have been possible. He knew where He needed us to be. All that I have been blessed with is possible because of Him.

Nikhom Bailey was born in Laos, a country in Southeast Asia. She is the daughter of Joe K. and Sy Vilaysouk. Raised in the city of Eagan, Minnesota, she served in the U.S. Marines for ten years. Now she is a homemaker and currently a student at a nearby college. She lives in Apple Valley with her husband, Jeff, and their four children. During her free time, she enjoys cooking, decorating, shopping, movies. and reading.

Growing
in the Spirit

BY TAMARA CLIFFORD

I'VE BEEN BLESSED with many experiences that have shaped my testimony and confirmed over and over again that my Father in Heaven loves me. As I thought about writing something for this book, I was unsure of what to share. Most of the sisters in our ward know of the loss of our son Jacob. That experience, though heart-wrenching, did provide some of the most powerful spiritual experiences of my life. The two precious months we had with him filled my life with chances for answered prayers and comfort from the Spirit, and the veil was indeed very thin during those days following his death. But for some reason I feel more inclined to talk about two other experiences I had that impacted my life greatly.

When I was 7 years old. my family moved from a small town in Utah to a big city in California. I was devastated to leave my friends behind but also excited to be close to family. One day my aunt Jill asked me if I would like to be in a play about the restoration of the gospel called the Oakland Temple Pageant. I was a bit of a ham as a kid and jumped at the chance to be a part of my very first play. I couldn't believe I would get to wear make-up and a costume! When we got to the interstake center in Oakland, I was put in a scene depicting the Savior visiting the Americas after his resurrection and in some of the pioneer scenes. I loved every minute of it. I learned all the music and did my best to play my part. On the night of our first performance I got to my spot in the opening scene, the orchestra began its intro, and then the balcony choir (made up of youth all dressed in white) began to sing, "Behold! I am the Law and the Light." My heart beat so fast as the actor portraying the Savior walked down some stairs and touched my face. I knew this person was a regular man pretending to be Jesus, but I also knew that I was feeling the Spirit in a way I had never felt before. I knew that Jesus Christ was the Savior of the world and He loved me. It was a powerful experience that I remember vividly as the beginning of my testimony.

The second experience I thought I would share happened many years later in the summer after my sophomore year at BYU. I don't want to give all the sordid details but suffice it to say my heart was completely broken by a boy. My engagement was off and I was a mess. I cried every day, didn't eat much, and was very confused. I thought I had been given an answer to prayer that it was okay to marry this man. If so, why did it end? I was hurt, embarrassed, and lonely. I prayed relentlessly to try to not be so sad and to understand what was going on. My parents had to watch me go through this and felt just as helpless as I did. (Although, years later, they told me they were *so* glad that engagement ended. They weren't the biggest fan of the guy.) Anyway, my parents' hearts were breaking right with mine as they watched me be sad.

After some time my dad offered to give me a blessing. We both cried through the blessing. I remember an overwhelming feeling of love from my Father in Heaven once again. I still didn't totally understand, but I knew that I wasn't alone, my prayers had been heard, and I was going to get through this. I was also powerfully reminded of the love of my dad. It gave me hope for a better tomorrow.

Things were still tough for me. My confusion of why I felt I had been given the answer of "yes, go ahead and marry this guy" and yet we broke up wasn't going away. But as days went by, more and more peace came. One day it came in the form of my mom's friend. She came up to me and said out of the blue, "You know, Tamara, the prophets have taught that most marriages can work if the couple stays true to their covenants and are faithful. Maybe Heavenly Father wanted to show you what a marriage to this guy would be like before you married him, and that's why it ended." She said this nonchalantly, and I don't think she ever realized that she was an answer to my prayers. She clarified things for me and made sense of everything. Yeah, I could have married that guy and I could have made it work, but I would have had to deal with a lot of garbage for the rest of my life.

Less than a month later I was back at BYU doing my laundry in the laundry room of my apartment complex when a tall, cute guy named Mike Clifford walked in and made me laugh. The worst summer of my life helped me to realize what was truly important in a man/husband, and then I met the most wonderful man who had all of those important traits.

I know through these experiences and through many others throughout my life that Heavenly Father hears and answers prayers. He loves each of us. He knows everything about us. He is merciful and kind. He will never leave us alone if we do our part to let Him into our lives.

Tamara Clifford moved to Apple Valley in 2007. She is the daughter of Gale and Maureen Westover and was born in Walnut Creek, California. She graduated from BYU-Provo in 2000 with a B.S. in sociology with a minor in business. She worked for a time as an H.R. manager and is now a stay-at-home mom. She has five children, the second of whom passed away when he was two months old. Raised in the Church, she has served in many callings in Primary, Relief Society, and Young Women's. She plays volleyball in a community league. She also enjoys board games, singing, and listening to good music.

The Incredible Job

BY ERIKA HOGGE

CONNECTICUT IS A LOVELY PLACE! The fall foliage is breathtaking and the summers feel quaint like the good ol' days. It was the perfect place to begin our life after graduating from college. Well that, and ConnDOT (Connecticut Department of Transportation) had offered Brian his first post-degree job. Our life was about to begin. We packed up our car, our 4-month-old baby, and after a tearful goodbye to family, we started on our journey to New England.

Eighteen months later, we were informed that the Governor was going to lay off three thousand state employees due to budget problems. We prayed and prayed that our family wouldn't be one of those affected.

I still remember hearing the keys in the door three hours too early one day. Brian had lost his job. He was able to finish out the month of December with ConnDOT before the layoffs which were effective January 1, 2003. We began to look for work, but we were devastated. We were young, poor, seven months pregnant, and had no family anywhere near us. What were we to do? We prayed.

It was about three weeks before Christmas when we heard about the job loss. Our parents had purchased plane tickets for us to come home for the holidays. It was a wonderful escape from reality to be with family.

While visiting Brian's family, Brian's father offered to give him a blessing. I still remember hearing the words: "Your Heavenly Father loves you and is preparing an incredible career opportunity for you." Once the blessing was finished, I looked up only to see all our family members with tears in their eyes. Little did we know what the Lord had in store for us!

We returned home to Connecticut. About a week later Brian received a call from the University of Connecticut asking him if he would like to work for them. This was a swift and much appreciated answer to prayer. And although we were able to stay financially afloat, as well as have Brian's postgraduate classes paid for by the university, we knew that this was not the job mentioned in the blessing.

A few years later, Brian decided to apply for a job with the Federal Highway Administration (FHWA) in Michigan. It's not easy to get a job with the FHWA unless you're recruited out of college, but we had faith that the promise in Brian's blessing would be fulfilled. He passed the exam, and went through two rounds of interviews. Our fingers were crossed!

A few weeks later, Brian received a call from Michigan: "I'm sorry, Brian, but you didn't get the job." I tried to remain upbeat and positive for my sweet husband but was secretly heartbroken for him. Brian immediately called his dad to update him on the situation. I remember hearing Brian say, "I didn't get it, Dad." I felt so sorry for him. What I heard next confused me. "No, Dad, that's not going to happen." Huh? Then once again, "Well, Dad, I understand what you're saying, but I just don't understand how that could happen." When Brian hung up the phone he told me that his dad had said, "Nope, you got the job. They're going to call you back. The Spirit confirmed this to me." A few days before, Brian's sister, who lives in Michigan, had a very powerful spiritual experience. She was driving her car and had to pull over to the side of the road because she was overcome with the Spirit. The Spirit told her we were moving to Michigan. Brian's sister called her dad, and the Spirit confirmed to him that what she said was true. So when Brian called his dad to tell him that he didn't get the job, Brian's dad said that the only rational explanation was that they were going to call back and tell him he did, in fact, get the job.

Five days passed without any news. We assumed that Brian's dad and sister were mistaken. Why would they receive revelation for us, and why hadn't we felt or been whispered anything? We prayed again.

The next day the phone rang. I answered it only to hear, "Hi, I'm looking for Brian Hogge. This is Dave with the Michigan Division of the Federal Highway Administration." My jaw nearly dropped. I basically threw the phone at Brian and stood there eavesdropping.

Brian hung up, looked at me, and said, "We got it."

We don't know what exactly happened to change the "no" to a "yes," but we know Who was ultimately responsible. I remember us immediately falling to our knees in a prayer of gratitude.

"I know Heavenly Father loves each of us."
Erika Hogge, 2013

Brian called his father and sister, both of whom basically said, "We knew it."

Brian has worked for the FHWA for many years now. He absolutely loves his job, and we know *this* is the job we were told about in that blessing years before.

I know our Heavenly Father loves each of us. He is always looking out for us. And even though we have to go through trying situations, He is there for us. We just have to have faith, and sometimes rely on others to help us get through when we are lacking.

Erika Hogge loves to laugh and to speak in different accents. Her flair for drama and her love of theater have enabled her to perform in many college and community musicals. She was born in Provo, Utah, and has very loving and supportive parents. Erika attended Utah Valley University and now works as a stay-at-home mom and vocal instructor. She and her husband Brian have four children. They moved to Minnesota in 2009. Erika hates ice in any drink except Diet Coke and can name all the counties in Utah in under eight seconds.

SHOWING OUR FAITH THROUGH OBEDIENCE

A Tithing Miracle

BY SONIA GLASER

I STARTED PAYING MY TITHING long before I became a member of the Church. I knew in my heart it was the right thing to do and never questioned the pros and cons of this covenant. However, I didn't really realize at that time how great our Savior's love is and how willing He is to bless our lives.

One morning I found myself staring at my empty fridge pondering how I will survive one week without food. I had earlier in the day paid my tithing and all my bills, including my rent, to find out that I had only five francs and some change left. Not knowing what to do, I decided to turn my concern to Heavenly Father in prayer. As I was just beginning my plea, a voice made itself heard in the room and instructed me to go to the store and buy the groceries I needed. In response I implied my doubt and reinforced the fact that I didn't even have enough to buy a loaf of bread or even a liter of milk. The voice patiently repeated the message, inviting me to go to the store and buy what will be needed only for this week. Skeptical but hungry, I obeyed, and I went thinking that the only shame I will have to endure will be me arriving at the cashier with a cart full of sustenance and telling her, "I am sorry, but I don't have any money to pay for all this."

But the Lord had a plan. I was walking from aisle to aisle and finally stopped at the deli to get some ham. As I was standing there waiting for my turn, a toddler sitting in one of the carts in front of me was throwing his toys on the ground. I would gather them up and give them back to him, which of course he tossed again. As I was kneeling one more time to pick up the toys, I noticed a tiny piece of paper barely visible stuck under the counter. I didn't pay too much attention to it, but the Spirit knew otherwise and whispered to me to retrieve it. As I pulled on it, I came to realize that it was not a regular piece of paper but indeed a bill of fifty francs. I was speechless. Tears started to roll down my cheeks as feelings of peace and warmth enwrapped my soul.

But the miracle didn't stop there. Still weeping tears of gratitude, I went to the counter to pay for my groceries. After scanning all my items, the cashier looked at me and asked for the amount, which came to exactly fifty-five francs and some change.

How could one have any doubt after such a miracle?

I have seen the hand of the Lord bless my life countless times. Every time the same feelings of peace and warmth bear witness as a testimony to me that our Father in Heaven is aware of us.

I know He lives.

Sonia Glaser was born in Crehange, France, the daughter of Charles and Marie Ange Therese Pertrot Simon. She met her husband, Marty, when he was serving in the U.S. military in Europe, and she joined the Church in 1990 in Forbach, France. She moved to the United States in August 1991 and recently became an American citizen. Sonia and her husband have four children.

Behold and lo, mine eyes are upon you, and the heavens and the earth are in mine hands, and the riches of eternity are mine to give.
Doctrine and Covenants 67:2

Tender Mercies
Follow Faith

BY AMY MEYER

MY LIFE IS NOT MADE UP OF GRANDIOSE MIRACLES. It is made up of tiny tender mercies that the Lord has blessed me with that have shaped and made me who I am today. There are many times when I look back on situations when I realize that the Lord truly led and guided my decisions and the decisions of others. One in particular has impacted my life and the life of my family.

There are many times when you listen to the prophet speak and you say to yourself, "Well, that doesn't apply to me." You are too scared or too prideful to take the counsel to heart and just try and test it in your life. I am lucky though. There are times in my past when I have followed small counsels of the Lord, giving me practice, so to speak.

Sean and I married young and I got pregnant right away. To me, following the counsel of the Lord not to wait to have a family felt like something Sean and I needed to practice in our lives. That commandment I could do. The trial came when my desire to gain an education conflicted with the counsel of the Lord for mothers to stay home. It was a counsel that I ignored for about two years.

Finally, once I got pregnant with our second child, I realized that staying home was something that I needed to do. I needed to put my faith in the Lord and take the leap. So I quit my job and put my education on hold. It was scary. How could we go from being a two-income family to one income, when that income was meager at best? The only thing we could do was put our faith in the Lord and hope He would guide us.

I am here to say, almost four years later, that the Lord has not forsaken us. I look back and I can see the blessing that our family has received. The Lord did not desert us. He took us under His wing and led us. He taught me how to stretch a dollar. He helped us get our children the help they need from the school district for early intervention. He helped us start small and work our way up. The best lesson He taught us, though, was how to have faith and practice that faith. The gospel isn't a buffet where you can walk up and pick and choose what you want. If you do, you are keeping yourself from the full blessings of the Lord. He will bless you when you follow His commands, but when you try to practice them all, you will be showered with blessings.

The Lord loves each of us and will be with us, every step of the way.

Amy Meyer has developed "couponing" to a high art form. With the right coupons she can take home hundreds of dollars' worth of groceries for pennies on the dollar, and she readily shares this skill with friends. Amy was born in Fort Belvoir, Virginia, to Dan and Joanne Linnabary. After her parents were divorced, she gained Jim McCabe as her stepfather. Amy has four years of college. She is a stay-at-home mom who helps her husband, Sean, run his small business. They have three sons and Amy has begun home schooling their oldest.

Who knoweth not in all these that
the hand of the Lord hath wrought this?
Job 12:9

The Hot Tub Modesty Test

BY ANNA PUGMIRE

WE HAD A CLOSE FRIEND in Colorado. At her birthday party everyone wanted to go in her hot tub. The only problem was no one had a swimsuit. Our friend's mother told us, "Just go in nude." Once Allie and I figured out what she meant, we were shocked.

We wanted to go into the hot tub with the other girls, but we had been taught to respect our bodies and be modest. So we got up our courage and asked her mom for swimsuits. After we did that, I was scared that she would have no swimsuits that were modest. Luckily, two of our three choices were modest—an answer to our prayers.

The rest of her party was fun and exciting. I was glad that the Lord gave me the courage to stand for the right.

Remember, you can do fun things even while doing the right. It is actually more fun if you do what is right. I speak from experience.

Anna Pugmire attends Falcon Ridge Middle School where she will enter eighth grade in the fall. She swims and plays soccer and basketball. She also plays the violin. She would like to go into photography. Anna was born in Sandy, Utah, and has a twin sister named Allie. Their parents are Jeff and EmRee Pugmire. The family moved to the Apple Valley Ward in August 2011.

The voice of rejoicing and salvation is in the tabernacles of the righteous: the right hand of the Lord doeth valiantly.
Psalm 118:15

A Lesson on Service

BY BECKY WHITE

I was 18 and a freshman in college. There was a lesson on service at church one Sunday. The teacher must have encouraged us to pray for service opportunities because that is what I did. The next day I was walking to K-Mart a few blocks from my dorm. There was an extremely busy four-way stop intersection. As I was approaching the intersection, I saw a man and his two young children coming towards me in the crosswalk. The dad was in a wheelchair, and young son and daughter were riding their bikes. The little girl fell off of her bike in the middle of the road. The dad was unable to help her up. She was crying. For a moment it was a very stressful situation. The little boy tried to help his sister while trying not to fall himself. The cars anxiously waited for them to get out of the way. I don't think they saw me coming towards them because, as I reached down to help the little girl up, the son and dad had a surprised and relieved look on their faces. I quickly helped her up on her bike and across the street. I was told thank you a hundred times in that little moment.

It was such a small and simple thing that I did, yet I know it meant a lot to that family at the time. I am so thankful Heavenly Father answered my prayer by putting me in the right place at the right time. That experience was small but meant a lot to me. It made me feel good inside to have helped someone, and it strengthened my testimony that Heavenly Father loves *all* of us and answers our prayers.

Becky White enjoys spending time outdoors camping and taking road trips with her family. She and her husband, Mike, have two children. Becky is a registered nurse and works at Abbott Northwestern Hospital. She was born in Caledonia, Minnesota, grew up in Faribault, and moved to Apple Valley nine years ago. Her parents are John and Patty Reher.

The Lord Blesses Those Who Strive to Serve Him

BY ASHLEY FLAKE

WHEN I WAS ABOUT 10 YEARS OLD, I had an experience that showed me the Lord blesses those who strive to serve Him. Here is a journal entry that I found on this experience:

"A couple of days ago I had a Flip's [gymnastics] competition. It was on Saturday, October 25, 2008. I did great! I think one reason I did good was because on Monday, October 20, 2008, instead of going to gymnastics, I went to activity days [a weekday Primary activity for girls ages 8 to 11]. That day after school my mom let me decide if I wanted to go to gym, or if I wanted to go to activity days. I decided to go to activity days. I told my mom that I thought that Heavenly Father would help me if I went to activity days instead of gymnastics. I was right! I did awesome! I got first on Vault, first on Bars, fourth on Beam, second on Floor, and first in the All Around. I think that Heavenly Father helped me that day."

As I looked back on this experience, I realized that the hand of the Lord was in my life at that time. I wanted to do what was right, and I knew that Heavenly Father would help me in my gymnastics competition if I did what was right.

I think that the Lord blesses those who put their *whole* trust in Him, and in this experience, He showed His love for me. I *fully* believed that He would make up the difference for me, and I know that mattered to the Lord.

Ashley Flake moved to Minnesota with her family in August 2012. She will be a sophomore at Apple Valley High School in the coming school year. She loves participating in gymnastics, ultimate Frisbee, dance, and choir. She also likes being with her parents, Maury and Lisa Flake, and her three brothers. Ashley was born in Corvallis, Oregon.

Listening to the Spirit

Water
in the Desert

BY KOURTNEY MARIE GRAHAM

IN AUGUST OF 2006, when I was about 9 years old, my immediate family went to Washington to spend time with my mom's mom for Cody's baby blessing. My dad's mom and dad also came to Washington to be there for Cody's blessing, but also because the children were going to go home with them. We were in the middle of moving to Utah, and my parents needed someone to take us so they could finish packing boxes and not have to run after kids everywhere. I remember finishing up the evening with my cousins and extended family before we all piled into our minivan to leave with my grandparents. Right before I left, I had this urge to go and get a couple of water bottles. I didn't really realize it was the Spirit talking to me, so I just went along with it and grabbed two Dasani water bottles from my grandmother's house. When I got back to the car, I tucked them in under my seat and forgot about them.

We spent a couple of days driving, enjoying the beautiful mountain scenery when we weren't driving my grandparents cra-

Before our car trouble, we were having a great trip with our grandparents. We stopped by a mountain lake, and Gerritt and I got out to stretch our legs.

zy, vegetating on electronics, or killing each other. Eventually, we finally reached the Nevada state line and were so excited because we were so close to Nan and Poppa's house. However, a couple of miles outside of Las Vegas, near a little town called Indian Springs, our minivan decided it had had enough and broke down in the sweltering desert heat. As my grandparents tried to find out what was wrong and see if they could get a call to my family somehow, we kids wandered the area adjacent to the side of the road, though I eventually went back to the car because of the heat and my fear of snakes. Before we had all gotten out of the car, my grandma said a prayer that the Lord would help us and that we would be able to make it home safely, and I kept asking my grandma why the Lord wasn't magically fixing the car. She said that the Lord works in mysterious ways and that we had to be patient and see what happened.

What seemed like an eternity later to a 9-year-old, two cars pulled off to the side of the road to see what was wrong. One car went to get a tow truck, though he never returned, and the other stayed behind to help my grandfather start the car. The minivan came back to life and we were back on our way, thanking the man for his help. However, the desert heat had leeched most of the water out of my brothers and they were desperately thirsty. But all of our water was gone, and we were still a good distance away from any place that could give us water. It was then that I remembered that I had those two water bottles tucked away under my seat, and even though they were plenty warm, they were able to help satisfy my brothers' thirst long enough for us to reach the army base right outside Las Vegas.

One thing you have to know about army bases is that they are *strict*. Normally, on my grandparents' cars, they have a special sticker that lets them in without having to pull out all of that paperwork to verify who they were, but my parents' car didn't have that. My grandfather had all of his paperwork out and ready so that we could get through faster, but when we pulled up, the guard simply let us pass without looking at the paperwork. My grandmother burst into tears, and after we got the water we so needed, we bowed our heads in prayer and thanked the Lord for helping us get home safely.

It wasn't until much later that I learned my grandparents had been able to patch one call through in the middle of a desert with no cell phone coverage to my parents. They were able to tell them that we were in trouble before the connection broke, and my parents spread the word that we needed prayers. Not only did we have our own prayers, but the prayers of my family reaching heaven as well.

 This story has always stuck with me and is one of my very earliest experiences with miracles and the Lord answering prayers, and is close to my heart as a result. Miracles don't always have to be fire from heaven. They can be just a couple of water bottles and the softening of hearts.

Kourtney Marie Graham recently graduated from Apple Valley High School and will be attending BYU-Idaho in the fall of 2013. She enjoys studying Japanese language and culture. Swimming, drawing, and hanging out with friends are high among her preferred activities, but most of all she enjoys writing and hopes someday to be a successful author. She was born in Safford, Arizona. Her parents are Darren and Heather Graham and she has five younger brothers.

Blessed for Following A Prompting

BY CAROLINE KORTH

WHEN KEN WAS FINISHING his bachelor's degree at Brigham Young University, we lived at Wymount Terrace. In January Ken was assigned a new home teaching family named the Smiths, who were both from Georgia. They had just gotten married a few months earlier and were new to our BYU married ward. Ken had the opportunity to home teach the Smiths only one time when we learned the husband, Doug, had been diagnosed with lymphoma, a form of cancer. He was only 23 years old.

Ken was very faithful about visiting Doug and his wife, Amy, and was given the opportunity to bring the sacrament to him while he was in the hospital. Doug spent the next several months in the hospital, and had some very tough times. In May Ken left for a six-week internship in New York City, and I stayed behind in Provo. Ken stayed in touch with Doug and Amy while he was in New York.

THE HAND OF THE LORD

Beyond introductions, I had not spoken to the Smiths much at all. I don't remember all the specifics, but I do remember while Ken was in New York, every time I left my apartment I would look over at the Smiths' home. I felt prompted to go visit them, or at least call and see how they were doing. I fought these promptings. It seemed like the more I fought these promptings, the louder they became. For some reason the Holy Ghost wanted me to befriend Amy and Doug, and I did not understand why. After about a month into Ken's internship, he called tell me some good news. Doug was in remission, and the doctors declared him cancer free.

Although Ken was elated, my feelings were very reserved. I had very strong feelings about death; I was very afraid of it. I wanted no part in it, and now Ken had formed a relationship with this couple and was planning on going tubing and having picnics together. All I could think about in the back of my mind was that Doug might die. When Ken returned from his internship, we had some picnics and fun times together with the Smiths. With Doug's cancer in remission we would get together and talk about the future. I still could never shake the feeling that Doug was going to die. However, I did eventually open my heart to Amy, and I started to feel connected to her.

The next part happened very quickly. One night Amy called to tell us Doug was not feeling very well. Within a few hours he became very ill and Amy said she needed help. Without any hesitation I ran over to help. I think somewhere in the back of my mind I knew this could be the end. Yet, I was fearless. All my fears about death were gone. By the time we got to the hospital, it was evident that the time for Doug to return to our Heavenly Father was very close, if not already here. He died that morning. In the weeks and months following his death the veil was very thin. Amy and I spent many hours sharing our feelings about death and the resurrection. We cried together and lifted each other up.

Looking back now, I realize this was a turning point in my life. My feelings about death were changed forever. Amy was able to help me face something very scary, and I in turn was able to help Amy face her darkest fears. Together we were stronger and our testimonies grew. Promptings sometimes come quietly to my heart, but if they get loud and strong, I know it's time to act. We are all tools in God's plan and we need to put our faith in God for He knows the way.

Caroline Korth was born in Detroit, Michigan, and she is the daughter of Karen Giacalone and Dale Hoekstra. She holds a B.A. in English from BYU and has worked for the past four years as an educational assistant in a special education classroom. Before that, she was a stay-at-home mom for her two children. Raised in the Church, she has served in many callings in the Primary and Young Women's organizations. She and her husband, Ken, moved to Minnesota in 1997 after he finished his degree. Caroline enjoys reading, watching movies, making crafts, and spending time with family and friends.

A Prompting in the Night

BY JACQUELYN A. KELLINGTON

I CAN'T SAY WHAT TIME IT WAS when I was awakened. The prompting was clear; it was strong. I was to give the pamphlet addressing the Restoration to three specific families. I thought about it for a time, wondering if it was really a prompting from the Spirit or just me. I did know it was not my style. I don't go around handing out pamphlets. So I went back to sleep.

Awakened a second time, the same prompting, only stronger. I was to give Restoration pamphlets to three specific families with whom I was acquainted. (Again, that's not my way of sharing the gospel.) I turned my thoughts elsewhere, desperately trying to capture sleep somewhere between then and daybreak.

I must have been successful, because being awakened for the third time was startling, even abrupt as the prompting was repeated for the third time. It was so clear, a voice in my head. I was to give to the three families the pamphlet declaring the Restoration. In my heart and in my mind I knew what I had to do. I conceded. If this was what the Lord wanted from me, then who was I to question? I could easily pick up the pamphlets in church on Sunday.

I keep my scriptures on the end of the dining room table, a reminder to read them daily. I try. That particular morning, as I sat down to read, amazingly sitting next to my scriptures were the three pamphlets I had been urged to give to the three families. I questioned everyone in the house. Had anyone for some reason placed the pamphlets next to my scriptures? Each responded they knew nothing of them. If there still had been any doubts or reservations in my mind as to the prompting, certainly they were now gone.

I considered the timing. When should I do it? I felt I should not put it off. Although a bit nervous, I did experience a sense of excitement considering what the outcome might be.

Gina, my neighbor, was a very loving and kind person. I always sensed a special spirit about her. Although strong in her own particular faith and church, she accepted the pamphlet graciously and with some enthusiasm. I felt I recognized a bit of curiosity in her and thought she might read it.

The second family, strong also in their faith, had very strong ties to their church. I remember clearly being touched by the sweetness of the children who drew pictures and gave them to me before I left. They were of a spiritual nature. Their mother was very sweet and respectful. As I explained my reason for being there, her respect remained as she asked if I had considered that my promptings could be Satan-based. She did, however, accept the pamphlet. I left their home feeling a bit discouraged and doubted she would read it, but then, who am I to judge?

The third family was a delight. I received a most warm welcome, even a hug. Gail and I had become friends long ago. We had on many occasions spoken of things of a spiritual nature. Their family has since moved, and I have had no contact with them for some time. I miss Gail's sweet spirit. I shared with her my experience that day. She did not doubt it. She was enthusiastic, accepting the pamphlet. She had, however, been thinking about temple work, something I had shared with her in the past. At that time she was not able to do this work herself and requested that I take the records of her parents and grandparents and arrange for their temple work to be done. I did and gladly! A brother in our ward who is a genealogy enthusiast did extensive work on this line and even found Gail had a Mormon heritage. We arranged for the temple work to be done for several generations.

After the work was completed, I took the records back to show the family members. Gail had trouble finding words to express her gratitude. I could, however, read the words of gratitude in her tears.

I too find it difficult to express the gratitude I feel, even now as I write, for the Lord allowing me to be an instrument in His hands to further this great work. My great hope is it will in some way continue in each of the other two families. This *is* a great work, a true work and the Lord's plan for us to be together in the eternities. I know it. I testify to it and I am grateful to be able to do so.

Jacquelyn A. Kellington has a gift for meeting people and learning how special they are. She was born in Minneapolis, Minnesota, and joined the Church in 1963. She has served in many callings, including being a stake missionary and a temple ordinance worker. She is a trained dental surgery assistant and recognizes God's hand in directing her to this profession. She also worked as a certified foster care provider for hard to place children and as a nanny for many years. She developed a deep love for the children she cared for. Jackie and her husband, Chuck, have six children of their own. Her parents are John Russel and Hannah Morehead Hoffman.

Humble yourselves therefore under the mighty hand of God,
that he may exalt you in due time.
1 Peter 5:6

Learn, Listen, Walk

BY MERLE PRATT

"EVERY ACTION HAS A KEYNOTE; let Christ be that keynote to which your whole life is attuned." This saying is on the wall in our living room. It says a lot about how we look at life.

Let's look at tuning. When the orchestra first comes onto the stage, they begin to warm up and tune. Everyone is playing something different and it sounds like chaos and confusion. Then the concert master stands and points to the oboe (usually) to give everyone a single note (concert A). Then each section in turn copies and matches that note. Then as a final check that they are in tune, they will play the notes in the chord with concert A as the root note (A major). The notes in the chord are in harmony; when a note is played that is not in the chord, it is called dissonance. Harmony is created when the sound waves in each note are aligned with the other notes. Dissonance is created when those waves bounce off of each other. Harmony and dissonance play off each other and create music. There are so many different types of music and we all have different preferences. Even individually we like different music for different things and at different times in our life.

When we tune our lives with Christ, we are in harmony with Him and His teachings. Dissonance is a necessary part of life. There are difficulties and stresses that lead to a resolution that gives peace. We would not feel that peace if there had not been a conflict or dissonance. Dissonance is not wrong; it is what builds and develops the music. Often when we are practicing (hopefully not when we are performing), we make mistakes. Many are easily recognizable because the dissonance is so strong. Sometimes we recognize the mistake because we know how the piece is supposed to sound, and sometimes a mistake will creep in, and it takes another person to tell us that there is a problem.

In life we make mistakes. Sometimes we recognize them ourselves and we correct them. Sometimes we can feel that something is not right. Sometimes the Holy Ghost will guide us. When we focus on living in harmony with Christ, we can hear the Holy Ghost and He will help us to make the right choices. He helps us find that peace. The Holy Ghost can also tell us when something is a dissonance—a part of life that is meant to help us grow—or a mistake or a sin.

In music at the end of the piece there is a resolution. It is at that point that the music leaves us on the *tonic* (the home chord). It resolves and we can feel the finish. Even a person that is not musically trained will feel uncomfortable when a piece is left unfinished. It is very unsettling to end a piece without finishing the resolution. Try singing just the first three lines of "Twinkle, Twinkle Little Star" and then not finish it. You will finish in your mind or you will feel very agitated. Sometimes a piece of music will lead us far away from that home chord, and it makes the resolution even stronger.

When our son Aaron was about 12 years old, he and his friend Jeremy wanted to ride their bikes to Jeremy's grandmother's house. Jeremy had done this often and he wanted to get the leaves raked for her. Everything seemed like it was something that would be good, but something just didn't feel right to me. It felt out of tune, so I said no, and Aaron and Jeremy were not happy. Again, it looked perfectly logical and a good thing to do. I could not give them a reason; the answer was just no. Aaron became very angry with me. I normally would talk out the problem, but in this case I said, "Because I am the Mom and I said no." The rest of the day was not pleasant. That evening while watching the news we learned the reason. There had been a high-speed police chase right in the area and at the time that Aaron and Jeremy would have been there. A boy on a bike about their age had been killed. So many times we receive warnings and we never know how the outcome would have been different. Aaron asked me how I knew that they shouldn't be there. All that I could tell him was that the Spirit had told me. It was a great teaching moment for me and for Aaron. I learned that when the Spirit speaks, we should not override it with logic. Only on rare occasions did I use the phrase "because I am Mom" but when I did, the kids listened and accepted the decision. They learned to seek out the Spirit.

We need practice to hear the Holy Ghost and His promptings, but as we do we will become better at recognizing and heeding His promptings. When we are in tune, we can find that peace that we are all seeking.

I enjoyed my kids' teenage years. There were struggles, but they were involved in many different activities, and I could really see the great adults that they were becoming. One of the contentions that was difficult for me was when they went out with friends. I wanted to know where they would be and when they would be home. They saw this as controlling and a power struggle resulted. There became a pattern of contention whenever they would leave. It was somewhat complicated by that fact that fairly often their dad would show up to check on them. (I appreciated that, but they didn't!) One evening as this pattern began, a whole new approach came to mind. The Spirit said: "Ask them what time to worry about them and where should we come looking for them." What a difference it made! Amy was a senior in high school and was participating in theater. Of course, her dad would show up at rehearsals every once in awhile. One time they were building sets when he showed up. One of the guys gave Amy a hard time, saying, "Doesn't your dad trust you?" The teacher immediately responded to the guy, "He trusts her. It is you he doesn't trust." Amy felt better about her dad showing up. A few weeks later Amy was again at rehearsal. It was late, the teacher had left, and a few of the kids were just finishing up when they discovered that they were locked in. At first they were worried, but then one of them said, "It will be fine. Amy's dad will show up soon." And he was right.

Doctrine and Covenants 19:23 is one of my favorite scriptures. "Learn of me, and listen to my words; walk in the meekness of my Spirit, and you shall have peace in me." I *learn* by scripture study, church attendance, and talking with others. I *listen* by prayer, temple attendance and quiet reflection. I *walk* by covenants and service. It is the plan of happiness. We came to earth to learn for ourselves. We walk by faith and we can do so by listening to the Spirit. When I need peace in my life, I know that what I need to do is Learn, Listen, and Walk.

Merle Pratt describes herself as a retired stay-at-home mom, which means that her six children have grown up and now she enjoys her twenty-two grandchildren. Music has filled her life since she was a child. She was born in Tremonton, Utah, to Keith and Rheta Burnham. She moved to Minnesota with her husband, Reo, and their children in 1986. Born in the Church, she has served in many wonderful callings and is currently secretary to the St. Paul Minnesota Temple president. Merle also has her own quilting business, complete with a long-arm quilting machine, and is a member of the Minnesota Quilter's Guild.

Knowing the Tender Mercies of God

He Knew

BY CINDY SINGER

I GREW UP IN UTAH in an active Latter-day Saint home. I think my testimony of the gospel has grown little by little as I followed the commandments, prayed, studied the scriptures, and surrounded myself with family and friends who were a positive influence on me, as well as listening to great leaders in my youth. I have always known that this gospel is true. I know our Heavenly Father is aware of us and loves us. Sometimes we are blessed with little "love notes" from our Father in heaven (as someone once called them) where we feel as if He is, at that very moment, directly speaking to us.

My experience I would like to share was one of those moments. I was very pregnant with my third child, the usual miserable, achy, tired, and maybe a bit grumpy as expected when nine months pregnant. I had gotten my other two children and myself up and ready for church that morning and had made it through the first two hours. By the time the third hour (Relief Society), came around, I was exhausted and really wanted the comfort of my home, comfy clothes, and pillow! I sat in the very back row in the Relief Society room and contemplated how I could just sneak out the door, grab my kids and head home. I reasoned with myself that after all, surely Heavenly Father would understand, and no one would really blame me for this decision. I had every right to be as comfortable as I could possibly be (which really wasn't that comfortable at all). I did stay long enough though to hear the message from our Relief Society president who said something like this: "I don't know who this is for, but I feel very strongly that our Heavenly Father wants me to stand up and say to you today that He is very aware of you and what you are going through and how you feel. He is happy that you are here and He loves you very much."

I really believe that this message was for me. It still brings tears to my eyes even to this day. I am grateful for a loving Heavenly Father, leaders who are able to be inspired to help others, and my testimony.

I love this Church!

Cindy Singer was born to Tom and Linda Rogers in Ogden, Utah, and grew up in an active LDS home. She has served in many callings, including Primary, Sunday School, and Young Women. She moved to Minnesota in 1990 where she met her husband Matt. Cindy works as a sonographer, or ultrasound technician, at a local hospital. She has three children and a lovely granddaughter. She is a runner and loves watching sporting events, especially when her children are participating.

The Lord Is There for Me

BY MARIA GANDARILLA

I JOINED THE CHURCH WHEN I WAS 14. My dad and step-mom introduced me to the Church. They kept inviting me and I kept telling them no. Then one day they said they could set it up for the missionaries to meet with me, and I gave in and said, "Sure." Shortly after that I joined. I just felt so welcome. Once they were doing a car wash at the church parking lot. It was a fun day. I still have a picture of it.

Now as a single mom, I feel Heavenly Father has been with me. He has given me strength when I've had my ups and downs. He was there when I didn't have a place to stay, and somehow some of my family that I hadn't talked to for a while came through. They opened their doors to me and let me stay there.

The Lord blesses me so that somehow it all comes out right, just daily things, personal things too. I just want my boys to continue going to Church. I know they will get lots of blessings following the Church and the commandments.

I was blessed to be in a ward with an active youth group when I joined the Church. This is the photo of the car wash activity the day I had so much fun as a teenager. I am standing in the back, the fourth person from the right.

Maria Gandarilla was born in Sunnyside, Washington. Her parents are Antonio Gandarilla and Guadalupe Rivera. She was living in Texas when she joined the Church, and she moved to Minnesota in 1995. She is a stay-at-home mom with three sons. She also studies part time and would like to be a nurse someday. Maria enjoys singing, dancing, and fishing, but not all at the same time.

Sad to Glad

BY ALLIE DARLENE PUGMIRE

YOUNG WOMEN'S CAMP was a life-changing experience for me. I turned 12 in 2012. To me turning 12 meant getting out of Primary and going to the temple. I paid little attention to going to Girls Camp, but when the time came to go, I was there and ready.

There were about nine hundred girls, plus their leaders and guest speakers. I shared a room with a girl who hadn't been baptized yet. I am glad that she allowed me to be part of her life and share this experience. We read our scriptures every day and said our prayers together.

On the last day of camp we had a testimony meeting. During the testimony meeting the room got hot because there were so many tears. I can't believe all the trials we, the young women, go through. When someone was sharing her testimony, I realized, for what seemed like the first time, all the blessings I've been given. Everything I have is a blessing. As my YCL (Youth Camp Leader) was sharing her testimony, she spoke about her older brother and what a great example he was to her as he experienced trials and always chose the right. I thought about my older brothers and realized what they had gone through. Like her brother, mine had always chosen the right. They have always been an example for me! I started to cry, as I realized what a jerk I was being at home.

With that realization I vowed to change my life. I became the happy, jumpy person I am today instead of the "Scowlie Allie" I used to be. I don't know why I wasn't this happy before. My life is full of joy, and I want others to feel that joy.

Allie Pugmire was born in Sandy, Utah, and is the twin sister of Anna. Their parents are Jeff and EmRee Pugmire. The family moved to the Apple Valley Ward in 2011. Allie is going to enter eighth grade at Falcon Ridge Middle School in the fall. She plays soccer and swims. She takes voice lessons and sings in the school choir. She also plays the piano. She would like to continue her studies in the musical arts.

Trust in the Lord

BY JESSICA ANN PETERSON

I WANT TO BEAR MY TESTIMONY about the power of hope and trust in the Lord. Many times throughout my life I have felt my Heavenly Father's compassion and His power.

One of those times I was working at a dude ranch in Arizona. I was 19 years old, and the ranch experience wasn't what I'd been told it would be. (If only I had a nickel for every time that happened.) I had been told the emphasis would be on performing, but instead I was doing a lot of dishes and cleaning. The rest of the crew (including my future husband) wasn't there yet, and I was very much alone. My mother wasn't thrilled with my summer plans. She didn't like that I was going to the dude ranch to save money to go to Zimbabwe. I heard about both experiences through others, and I signed up for them without knowing anyone else who was participating. She said she would agree to my plans if I got a blessing and it confirmed my decision. I received a blessing that stated I would be protected. It also promised several other things.

Jessica Kerr and Lance Peterson met on a dude ranch in Arizona. Shown here with a coworker (left), they sang and danced in country western shows to entertain ranch guests in the evenings.

One day I had a few hours off and went for a hike alone (not a wise choice). I was in the Arizona desert right behind the dude ranch and a mile from the Grand Canyon. I was hiking up some shale rock when I heard a hissing sound underneath me. While I climbed upward away from the rattlesnake, I kept slipping down toward the snake. He coiled. I said a quick prayer and in a split second reflected on my blessing. How could Heavenly Father promise protection and then allow me to get bitten while I was alone in a desert? A thought came clearly to my mind, "Do you believe me?" My heart confirmed to me that yes, I did believe Him. I was finally able to find some footing and get away far enough to look back at the snake slithering away.

I have learned through countless experiences that Heavenly Father loves me. Sometimes the snakes in my life have not gone away so quickly. Sometimes I wish for relief of a struggle and I simply continue to struggle. However, I receive hope and strength from prayer, from the faith and testimony of others, and from my Savior and my testimony of Him.

Jessica Ann Peterson was born in Lahr, Germany. Her parents, Paul and Anna Kerr, joined the Church while living there. Jessica earned a master's degree in social work from BYU-Provo in 1999 and has worked as a therapist in private practice since then. She, her husband, Lance, and their five children moved to the Apple Valley Ward in 2010.

Temple Flower Gardens

by Cara Marie Gordhamer

Ever since I was a little kid, I would go to do gardening at the temple grounds. I was always happy being there and loved learning how to garden. For me as a kid, it was fun and I got to go somewhere on a Saturday. Now I realize it was a tender mercy in my life. I realized it started a spark in my testimony. The temple is amazing, and I will treasure these experiences forever.

Cara Marie Gordhamer will enter Apple Valley High School in the fall. She is a native of Apple Valley and is the daughter of Shawn and Marlene Gordhamer. Along with gardening, she loves baking and thinks she may open a cafe someday. Meanwhile, she is going to study business and consider all possibilities.

Only with the Help of the Lord

BY SABRINA HERRMANN

WHEN I DIVORCED my first husband, I did not receive any financial support from him, and I had three children to raise. I went back to school at that time to get my degree as a registered nurse. I worked full-time doing data entry and also worked weekends doing a paper route to make enough money to provide for my family while taking two or three classes a semester.

The children were very busy. I had two in gymnastics and one of them was competing on the state team, and I was involved in traveling soccer. It took me six years to complete my degree, and many people cannot believe how I was able to do it all, but that is when the Lord carried me through.

I believe the Lord was by my side through what I consider to be one of my most difficult trials in life. Yes, I had many days where I would become discouraged and cry, but I always got through it. Knowing the Lord loved me and cared for me is how I made it.

Also many times I received help and guidance from God through other people. My brother and sister helped me by watching my children so I could go to class. My visiting teacher took my children to activities when I needed to be in two places at the same time, and the bishop took time to come to my son's soccer meets.

Sabrina Herrmann moved to Apple Valley when she bought her first home in 1994. She was born in Eau Claire, Wisconsin, and her parents are Ted and Shirley Aaron. Her first career was in data entry, and then she went back to school and received her RN, and shortly thereafter her B.S.N. She now works at Fairview Ridges Hospital. She was raised in the Church but became less active between the ages of 14 and 23. Currently she works at the temple and teaches in Primary. She has taught in Primary several times, has been Relief Society compassionate service coordinator, and has worked in Relief Society as a teacher. She has three children, Rick, Crystal, and Cassandra. Sabrina enjoys crocheting and loves to go to the movies and eat buttered popcorn. She also enjoys the outdoors and going for walks with her two dogs.

The Lord Is Watching over Me

BY VICKI MCGREGOR

I HAVE FELT THE HAND OF THE LORD in my life many times. Just last week, my husband, Ian, and I drove out west to visit my dad. We came back through Montana and North Dakota, something we have never done before. It turned out to be the only place in the country with blue skies and dry roads. South of our route were blizzards, snow, wind, and even farther south, tornadoes and other severe weather! Definitely the hand of the Lord.

A little over two years ago, I fell in ballet class, broke my foot, and sprained my ankle. Just for the record (insert old and fat jokes here) after nearly fifty years of classes, this was only my second injury in ballet. In my life, it was my first broken bone and my first sprained ankle! I was on crutches for several weeks. Over the next three months, I saw my doctor frequently for x-rays and checkups.

It so happened that I was also having some unrelated, troubling symptoms. Since I was going to be at the doctor's office, I decided I would ask her about them. At first her response was just try this, try that, no big deal. But after three months, she finally said, "This has gone on too long. You need to see a specialist."

Within a few weeks, I was diagnosed with cancer. My treatment started very, very soon after that. It was "one of the worst treatments we have." Nearly two years later, there is "no sign of cancer," although I still have debilitating side effects from the treatment. These should eventually lessen and, I hope, go away.

Where is the hand of the Lord in this? Our daughter, Amelia, who doesn't go to church right now, is convinced that breaking my foot and spraining my ankle saved my life. I don't know that I would have gone to the doctor so soon for the troubling symptoms I was having. Since I was there every few weeks anyway, the diagnosis came before it was too late.

After the diagnosis, there were tests to see the extent of the cancer and if it had spread. While I was drinking the "contrast" for two hours before the first CT scan, I prayed to Heavenly Father. I said that, if we found that the cancer hadn't spread, and if it could be cured, I promised that Ian and I would go on a mission. Then I chuckled a little. I know Heavenly Father has a sense of humor. We've been planning for a long time to go on a mission anyway.

I know that God lives. He hears our prayers and He answers them. I know that Jesus is the Christ. I am grateful that He suffered for our sins and tribulations. I am thankful for a living prophet on the earth today. I am thankful for the gospel and that the Church was restored in these latter days. And I am thankful for the hand of the Lord in my life.

Vicki McGregor was born in Salt Lake City, Utah, and at age 1 year went to Germany with her parents, Herold L. and Mary Ethel Eccles Gregory, when her father was called to preside over the East German Mission. She majored in German at the University of Utah and continues her interest in the language. She also studied ballet at the university on a four-year scholarship, and although she did not pursue a career in ballet, she still enjoys ballet classes. Vicki loves music and sings in the choir of a Presbyterian church. She has volunteered in the schools since 1986, and when she is at home, she reads and works intricate needlepoint designs on blank canvases, carefully counting out the patterns. She and her husband, Ian, have three children and two grandchildren. She is a temple worker and looks forward to serving a mission with her husband.

Behold, the Lord's hand is not shortened, that it cannot save; neither his ear heavy, that it cannot hear.
Isaiah 59:1

My Miracle Husband

BY NANCY GAYDER

MY HUSBAND, STEVE, hadn't been feeling well, so was lying in bed. Around suppertime I went to check on him and he was comatose. I called 911 to come get him, and I followed behind in my car. In the emergency room twelve or more medical staff crowded around him, working feverously. I stood in the corner watching.

The lead doctor called to me and brought me into another room. I crossed the room putting my back against the far wall, wanting to be as far away from the doctor as I could. She started by apologizing and then told me my husband had less than two hours to live—he had a bleed on his brain. I slid down the wall to a sitting position on the floor. She asked if I wanted to call someone.

I called my dearest friend, Mark, a priesthood holder from my ward. While waiting for Mark, the hospital staff took me to a small private room with a television, two love seats, coffee, water,

Nancy Gayder: "My Miracle Husband" 175

soda and cookies. I sat. I sat. I sat. *Two hours? Two hours? What is there to do? What am I going to do?*

Mark finally arrived. His opening remark was, "Nancy, he's grey. He needs a blessing."

We called the bishop who was more than willing to come to the Emergency Room. The three of us walked over to Steve's room. A full medical team was still working on him. I had to ask some staff to move so that the blessing could be administered.

At that very moment, Steve's personal physician called and needed to talk to me. I missed the whole blessing! I don't even know who anointed or who blessed, not that it was that important, but I don't know.

The three of us walked back to the little waiting room, leaving Steve in the same state he was in when we arrived. I, of course, was still sobbing. I looked at the two priesthood holders and asked if my husband was going to die. They told me they had not released him to go.

An instant relief rushed through my neck and shoulders. I felt a total relaxation. I knew with certainty he would live. The blessing spoke to that. A smile crossed my face.

At that moment we heard a voice. The men looked at me, each with a grin. I said, "Yes. That's Steve."

Hospital workers were pushing Steve on a gurney, and as he went past our room, he waved his arm and said, "Hi, Bishop. See you Sunday." The doctor popped her head in and said they were going for another brain scan.

The brain scan was perfectly clear. The doctor said she couldn't explain it, but everything was fine.

Steve came home the next day and was in church on Sunday, just like he said!

Nancy Gayder passed away on May 2, 2013, while this book was in production. Before her last illness she contributed this story and one other. She was a member of the Apple Valley Ward less than two years, and made many new friends here while retaining close ties with friends in the Farmington Ward. Nancy was born in St. Paul, Minnesota, the daughter of Kenneth and Edith Dunn. She joined the Church in 1982. Before her retirement she worked as an accountant in an insurance firm. She loved people, dogs, crossword puzzles, and Disney movies. Because of her last name, she also liked to collect things with an alligator motif.

Our
Miracle Baby

BY KRISSY SCHWEIGERT

A TIME WHEN I SAW THE SAVIOR'S HAND in my life was during the pregnancy and birth of our eldest child Haley. When Chad and I became pregnant with Haley, we were ecstatic. We told all of our friends and family around the twelve-week mark, and everything was going along fine until I reached fourteen weeks.

We were at my mom's house celebrating the holidays. All of a sudden my water broke. We all knew this was a terrible thing as I was only fourteen weeks along. As my mom and husband frantically drove me to the emergency room, I was upset, but I felt quite calm and sensed a small voice telling me everything was going to be all right. I am normally a person who would have panicked and been very upset, but a calm came over me that I had not experienced before. I was taken to the hospital where they told us that the baby was all right at the moment but that I would probably suffer a miscarriage. I was sent home to go on bed rest until I could see my doctor.

THE HAND OF THE LORD

When I saw him a few days later, the baby was still all right but he told us to not get our hopes up. I had a continual leak of amniotic fluid which is needed to help develop the lungs of the baby. Lungs cannot be seen on the ultrasound, so we would not know if the baby had lungs until she was born. The doctor told us that we could proceed with the pregnancy or terminate (which he recommended), as the prognosis was not a good one. The baby had about a ten percent chance of survival. The idea of a termination was not even an option in our eyes, so we proceeded with the pregnancy.

I spent weeks fourteen to eighteen at home on bed rest. Although I was frightened and worried, I continued to feel the quiet calm voice telling me all would be well. At eighteen weeks I was admitted into Abbott hospital. I had a wonderful doctor who specialized in high-risk pregnancy situations. She saw me daily in the hospital, and every time she came to my room, she would say, "I have a good feeling about this one!"

I spent the next fourteen weeks on bed rest in the hospital having ultrasounds every three to four days, with lots of poking and being hooked up daily to the heart monitor for the baby. Each day I prayed for the safe and healthy delivery of our sweet baby girl. I continued throughout this time to feel the calm and small voice telling me everything would be all right. I had many wonderful friends and family who came and visited me in the hospital, helping make getting through each day a little easier.

On May 2, 2000, I went into labor in the morning. I was thirty-two weeks along. I prayed as I started labor. I knew it was still early to deliver the baby. I knew the longer she stayed in my tummy the better chance her lungs had of developing. I asked

Heavenly Father to please let me go just a few more weeks to give her the best chance. While praying I heard that small voice telling me everything would be all right. This was the time that she was supposed to come.

That afternoon I delivered a beautiful baby girl, weighing 3 pounds, 7 ounces. When she was first delivered, they had trouble getting her to breathe. She was turning purple and had to be hooked up to a breathing tube. As I lay there watching them trying to get her to breathe, I panicked and began to pray. Again the same voice told me that everything would be fine. That same calm came over me and I felt at peace. Eventually they got her to breathe. She was on a ventilator, but she was breathing.

Over the next few weeks we watched her go from the Neonatal Intensive Care Unit to the Special Care Nursery to home. It was a long hard road even when she came home. She needed special care and had spells of turning blue and stopping breathing. Through all this I continued to feel the calm telling me all would be all right.

Our sweet baby girl just turned 13! It is a miracle that she is here with us. I know the feeling of calm and the whisper that everything would be all right through the entire pregnancy was my Heavenly Father helping me. I know there is no way we could have gotten through this experience without that calming voice telling me everything would be all right. I also know that our beautiful girl would not be with us today if it were not for our Father in Heaven watching out and protecting her.

I am so grateful for this experience. It has taught me so many things that I needed to learn. I also know Heavenly Father gives us experiences that we need to have. More than anything I know

Haley, now age 13, is living proof that miracles do happen and that Heavenly Father answers prayers.

now more than ever that Heavenly Father truly cares for each of us and knows exactly what we need and when we need it. He is there for each of us through all of our ups and downs. He was there and helped me feel calm and to know everything would be all right. I will always be thankful for that calm feeling and still small voice that helped us get through this experience.

Krissy Schweigert was born in Edina, Minnesota, and was baptized at age 11 when her family was living in Germany. Her parents, David Nordstrom and Diane Johnson, are divorced. Krissy and her family moved to the Apple Valley Ward in 2013 to live with her mother while her husband, Chad, completes his education. They have two children. Krissy is a stay-at-home mom who loves to scrapbook, take pictures, and play the flute. She is a leader for Haley's Cadet Girl Scout troop. Most of all, she loves being with her family.

Frankie

BY DANNICA DUFUR

ON JULY 18, 2012, I had to watch one of the most important things in my life be handed back to God. My family's 2-year-old bulldog, Frankie, suffered for nine months from epileptic seizures that no amount of medication or prayer were able to cure. Around the time the seizures first started my sister and her husband found out that they were expecting their first child.

Daily I prayed for his peace and comfort as he struggled to find a new normal through the haze of medications and multiple seizure episodes. With every medication there was a new hope that this would be the one, but even after every pill concoction the vets could come up with, we still had no answers. There were x-rays, blood samples, pokes and prods, and still the seizures continued. We began to feel selfish when we understood the extent of his suffering as he tried to remain our faithful friend. Slowly but surely, a realization settled over us that the end was near. We would all need to start to find our peace with having a special element of our lives go home.

Our bulldog, Frankie, brought us so much joy. We believe his unconditional love was a gift from our loving Heavenly Father.

A decision was reached that after the next round of seizures our beloved dog would finally be put to a restful sleep. Waiting for the seizures was hard, but meanwhile we all prayed for the best outcome for him. We weren't thinking of ourselves anymore, and that is when Frankie decided it was time.

On July 18, 2012, he had a grand mal seizure and was taken to the hospital to be relieved of his suffering. There are no words to describe the pain that we felt having to let our buddy go, but we knew he had fulfilled his purpose in life.

Tears still come daily; his presence is always missed but we can see him, running around, pain free and in his own heaven. After many prayers and a special blessing from the Pugmire family, life started to move forward again. Less than two months after Frankie was put to sleep, our family was blessed with a different type of gift from God—a baby girl named Elouise. We realized that it was a blessing from God to have the burden of Frankie's illness lifted from us so we could prepare for the new life He was sending into our care.

Without the knowledge that the Church has blessed me with throughout my life, I do not know if I would have been able to accept letting Frankie go. I know that someday I will be able to kiss his nose and watch him perform his tricks when I go home. Every thing in this life has a reason and a purpose; Frankie's was showing us unconditional love and laying the foundation for a new baby's life.

Dannica Dufur was born in Parkston, South Dakota, because that's where the hospital was. Her parents, William Richard and Regina Dufur, lived in Wagner, South Dakota, at the time and that's where she was raised. In 2007 Dannica moved to Minnesota to attend Southwest Minnesota State University where she earned a B.A. in literature and creative writing with a minor in history. Upon graduation in 2011, she came to Apple Valley. She works full-time as a client services representative and part-time at Mall of America. She is an avid reader and enjoys crocheting blankets.

He Sends Angels to Lift Us Up

BY JOSALYN McALLISTER

MY HUSBAND AND I HAVE LEARNED to seek the guidance of the Lord. We have made everything a matter of prayer from what we should study in school, to which job we should take and where we should move, when we should have our children, and how we should structure our family life. We have confidence that because we have been obedient to the Lord's counsel in the scriptures and through modern prophets, He will guide us to the places we need to be. It has been an adventure that has taken us far away from our families and comfort zones, but the blessings we have received have been innumerable. Although we often miss our extended families, especially in times of crisis, we have trust that the Lord will take care of them as He has taken care of us.

Our first major move, from Utah to Kansas, started when our first baby was only four days old. We didn't know a single person in Kansas, but my husband had a job there upon graduation from

BYU. I was still recovering from delivery and, when we got to our new home, our baby had spent half of her little life on the road. I was used to teaching junior high school students, constantly talking to people, and always having a million things to do. Adjusting to a new place, to being a new stay-at-home mom, and to learning how to take care of a new baby was a little overwhelming, but we were excited and confident we would be able to overcome our challenges. We arrived at our new home on Monday night, and David went to work the next morning. I foolishly spent the day unpacking and ended up on my back by mid-afternoon. (I didn't realize what recovery meant.)

David came home from work that day to report that the Mormons at the office had already found him. Shortly after that I got a call from the local Relief Society president who had arranged meals and visits for us for the next two weeks. I am so grateful for her for not waiting until Sunday to meet us, that she didn't think to herself, "I have done enough for today." I am certain that she followed the promptings of the Spirit. When she heard that we had had such a big move, she was filled with compassion for me. I love that woman. I think of her whenever I hear the phrase "comfort those who stand in need of comfort." There were many other wonderful people who opened their homes to us and who taught me how to survive having an infant. That ward will always have a special place in our hearts because of how much we needed and relied on them, and how warmly they received us. We have been trying to pay it forward ever since.

I am so grateful for the gospel of Jesus Christ. I am grateful that He teaches us to love and serve one another in His stead. I am also grateful for the organization of the Church, that no matter where we go we have family who will look out for us and take care of us. I am also grateful the Lord is mindful of us. He knows our needs and sends angels to lift us up.

Josalyn McAllister and her husband, David, moved to the Apple Valley Ward in April 2013. She was born in Santa Barbara, California, and is the daughter of Wayne and Heidi Baldwin. She graduated from BYU and taught history in a junior high school until her children were born. She is now a stay-at-home mom with three little girls.

Thy right hand, O Lord, is become glorious in power.
Exodus 15:6

God Sent People to Help Me

BY HAYMANOT BALCHA

I WAS REALLY STRUGGLING WITH MY MARRIAGE, and I was sharing my worries with my friend Tschainesh. My friend brought me to her church. I liked the Church and I decided to join.

After that I was pregnant and I was all alone with my struggles. I then shared with my friend Ginger on how to cope with my struggles. Ginger was an angel that God sent to me. She helped me through my pregnancy, and I successfully delivered the baby safe and sound. The bishop helped me too, and now I feel redeemed and born again.

I really want to thank everybody for the help they offered when I was really in need. I cannot pay you back for the miracles you did to me, but God will reward you. You are now my family and I hope we all stay in touch as we wait to go to heaven to meet our Father. Thank you so much. I have no words to express how grateful I am. May God bless you.

That is my story.

Haymanot Balcha was born in Addis Ababa, Ethiopia, and came to the United States in 2001. Her father is Sambata Balcha and her mother is Ungedai. She was baptized into the Church in April 2012. She works part time caring for residents in a nursing home. She is studying hard to earn her GED (Graduation Equivalency Diploma) so that she can go to college. She works out every day. She loves spending time with her three children. She also loves singing and going to church.

Thou shalt also be a crown of glory in the hand of the Lord, and a royal diadem in the hand of thy God.
Isaiah 62:3

Thoughts from the Kitchen

BY MARLENE GORDHAMER

I KNOW THAT THE LORD IS MINDFUL OF US. He loves us and wants us to feel His watch care every day. He meets our daily needs in many ways. I'll tell you of a time when I was certain He met my "wants." It wasn't anything on a grand scale, just a simple rice cooker. I learned the Jesus loves me and will provide me with what I need, but I have to do my part first and have faith.

My experience with the principle of faith and the love of the Savior happened a few years ago when I was going to make some rice for supper—only to discover that the rice cooker was broken. I knew that buying a brand new rice maker would be expensive, so I began to look in the stores for one that was on sale. But that turned out to be a disappointment—even with the sale price, the rice cookers cost too much.

What's a mother with a mission to do? I went to the Goodwill store and other area bargain stores like Saver's and Unique to find a rice cooker! I thought for certain that I'd find what I was looking for there—no initial luck. Time passed and I put looking for a rice cooker on the back burner, and I made other meals for my family that didn't use rice. I didn't give up though. I knew that I would eventually find a rice maker I could afford.

One day, months later, I was out and about grocery shopping and decided to see what the Goodwill store had to offer. Lo and behold, there was my rice cooker, a brand new Tupperware rice steamer sitting on the shelf! It was a happy moment of discovery, and I quickly put it in my cart and I was off to the checkout feeling pretty good about my find.

We've continued to use that Tupperware rice cooker, and every time I make a meal that uses rice, usually Mexican, I am reminded that the Lord loves me and is mindful of my simple needs and wants. I learned to recognize the hand of the Lord in my life that day I found my rice cooker. Because of this experience, I am more aware of how He blesses me each and every day, and I love my Savior a lot more for it. May we all look for the blessings that come from the Lord because they are there in our lives. We just need to learn to recognize them. So, the next time you're cooking at the stove, remember this point—the Lord is mindful of you and loves you.

Marlene Gordhamer is an avid reader, a generous baker, a happy gardener, an all-weather walker, a hand-crafted arts lover, and a daughter of God. She loves shopping for bargains, and listening to Christmas music all year round. She is looking forward to the time when she and her husband, Shawn, can serve a mission together. Meanwhile, child-rearing and home have her full attention. She is the mother of three and has three grandsons as well. Marlene is a convert, baptized in 1986. She was born in Tracy, Minnesota, and is the daughter of Eugene A. and Norma E. Meyer.

The hand of the Lord was upon me, and carried me out in the spirit of the Lord, and set me down in the midst of the valley…
Ezekiel 37:1

The Lord Healed My Heart

BY JACQUELYN A. KELLINGTON

HOW COULD I FORGET? I couldn't! A bag. Brown. A grocery bag. Its contents? The entire possessions of three small children: Bobbie Joe, Scottie, and Celeste. They were standing the entryway of my Apple Valley home, brought by the county social worker.

How could I know that such a strong bonding would take root in their hearts and mine? But then, it was not the plan for them to be with us for three years. Their return to their mother was painful, even heartbreaking. Celeste clung to me while the social worker labored to coax her from my arms. Many tears. It was right, but their absence hurt—a lot!

After some time I decided to return to work and took a position organizing the Meals on Wheels program for the city of Apple Valley. It was okay, but I still missed the children and their involvement with my family.

One day a lull at work afforded me an opportunity to "kick back" in my little office and read the paper. I don't know why, but

I started scanning the want ads. I wasn't consciously looking for a change in jobs, but when I came across the day care and nanny jobs, I felt curious. Certainly after being employed by a professional association, a treatment home for hard-to-place children, I would be qualified to be a nanny. Not being serious, but definitely curious, I began to call a few numbers.

I caught one man at home. John was very enthusiastic about the upcoming birth of their first child. Beyond that he expounded even more on all the marvelous and special qualities of his wife, Molly. (I still wasn't sure I wanted to nanny, considering that I was still hurting from the absence of three small children, but I most certainly wanted to meet this Molly person.)

Setting a time to meet, I resumed my workday schedule. I wasn't really settled in the Meals on Wheels job. It just didn't feel right; it didn't fit. Approaching a job change carefully, I petitioned the Lord, who knew of my heartbreak, for guidance. Considering the many times He had given me guidance, I had faith He would somehow direct me again. Several days before my appointment to meet with John and Molly, I was given a most direct and vivid dream.

In my dream I drove to a house and parked at the curb. The house stood on a small hill. Walking up several steps found me at their front door, ringing the bell. They quickly answered their door and invited me into their home. With a glance I observed a dining room on the left, a family room on the right with a staircase dividing the two. I was invited into the family room where I was seated on a couch against the wall. I noticed that everything was very light in color, even white. The fireplace that held family pictures was white. A baby girl was placed in my arms and then I awakened. The dream was so real, so vivid. I don't usually dream, at least not that I can remember, but this dream I felt I'd never forget.

It was finally time to go and meet John and Molly. Arriving at their home, I parked my car at the curb. Recognizing their home from my dream caused a chill to go through my body, and then a strange sense of calm that quickly turned to excitement as I ascended the not few steps. I felt I knew what to expect. As I entered their home, everything was as I had observed in my dream. Dining room on the left, staircase dividing it from the living room, and yes, the fireplace was white.

The visit lasted for some time. Molly was indeed all that John had proclaimed and more. Obviously intelligent, but sensitive, beautiful and of course excited about the birth of their first child. As we talked, I knew it was right. Before leaving they said, "We'll call you and let you know." My impression was they had others to interview, but I knew without any reservation they would call and request my help with their new family. I don't know if Molly would remember, but she asked me what I thought she would have, a boy or a girl. I responded, "A girl." Meagan was born shortly after.

I came on board and remained as nanny for some sixteen years, during which time a second daughter, Charlie, was born. During these years I came to love the girls. It was easy. I was able to observe some wise and sensitive parenting. Their mom was very goal-oriented, and the needs of Meagan and Charlie were always forefront in her mind. Both girls became champion equestrians. Many ribbons from horse competitions adorned their bedroom walls. Meagan finished high school and went on to college in

England where she experienced much success. Her sister, Charlie, likewise finished high school and attended a college in California and also experienced much success.

I often think of that dream so long ago and wonder why. Why did the Lord direct me there? I can only conclude that the Lord was letting me know He cared and He put me in a place with people He knew I would love. As I cared for these two beautiful little girls, my heart began to heal from the loss of the three children who had been in my care for three years before returning to their natural mother. I will, of course, never stop caring about them and their welfare. Nor will I ever forget the years with Meagan and Charlie and their generous parents. Truly, it was a time of many blessings, and I remain grateful.

Jacquelyn A. Kellington has a gift for meeting people and learning how special they are. She was born in Minneapolis, Minnesota, and joined the Church in 1963. She has served in many callings, including being a stake missionary and a temple ordinance worker. She is a trained dental surgery assistant and recognizes God's hand in directing her to this profession. She also worked as a certified foster care provider for hard to place children and as a nanny for many years. She developed a deep love for the children she cared for. Jackie and her husband, Chuck, have six children of their own. Her parents are John Russel and Hannah Morehead Hoffman.

The Right Word
at the Right Time

BY EMREE M. PUGMIRE

I HAD GONE TO SEE A NEUROLOGIST about my MS [multiple sclerosis] around the last week of May 2012. I scheduled some appointments with another referred doctor, but I felt I should try to find a doctor closer to my home. I did some more research and found one in Burnsville, although there was little information about him.

When I went to see him, I told him I had five children and he said, "Oh you're like Ann Romney." I said, "In more ways than one. I'm LDS too!" He then asked, "Is there a temple in the Twin Cities?" I said yes and told him where to find it. I then told him that he could actually go into the temple in Kansas City as it was having its open house. I explained that members of the Church who didn't hold temple recommends and members of the community could attend this special event. He said, "I've been reading about it. That's how I know about temples. I've been looking at pictures of the celestial room, and what is an ordinance room?"

I had just been to clean the temple a couple weeks before, and while I was cleaning, I noticed the sign outside of the first room said "Instruction Room." I thought that was weird, as I had never heard an ordinance room called that before. But when he asked, I thought of that sign and told him, "Another name for it is 'instruction room.' It is where we go to receive instructions on how to return to our Heavenly Father."

He was very satisfied with that answer. I thought how kind it was for Heavenly Father to help me notice that sign so I had an answer for my doctor when I needed it. At my next appointment I took him a copy of the Ensign about temples. I was planning to take a copy of the Book of Mormon to my third appointment, but it was cancelled, as he had abruptly left that practice. I have no idea why he left.

On July 18 we went to the temple with Anna and Allie so they could to do baptisms for the dead for the first time. We had a wonderful experience. As it was over, I was going to change, and I stopped to look at the sign identifying the "instruction" room. I must have had a dumbfounded look on my face because a little temple worker sister asked, "Sister, are you okay? You look confused."

I said, "I'm very confused. Is this a new sign?"

"No."

"Has it always said 'Endowment Room'?"

"Yes."

"Is there any other sign in this temple that says 'Instruction Room'?"

"No."

I just couldn't believe the entire experience! I had had a full conversation with myself looking at that sign so I know it wasn't just a mistaken glance. I thought of how much the Lord loved Dr. Tang to give him the answer to his question. It was only a word, but the Lord had done so much to get me into the situation where I could share the right word at the right time. I felt so grateful to observe the Lord's amazing work. What a marvelous work it is!

EmRee M. Pugmire was raised on a sugar beet farm in Lovell, Wyoming. Her parents, Brent and Darlene Moncur, raised their six children to love working and love their family. EmRee graduated from BYU with a B.S. in Family Sciences and an M.S. in Marriage and Family Therapy. EmRee was thrilled to serve a mission in the Pennsylvania, Pittsburgh Mission. She married Jeff, the man who makes her laugh daily, and together they enjoy their five children. They moved to Minnesota in August of 2012 after determining they wanted their children raised in the Apple Valley Ward.

Drawing Closer to Our Loving Father

God's Children

by Helen Manar

I work at the Target store in Bloomington, and I am often asked, "Why don't you transfer to the Apple Valley Target? It's closer."

At the Bloomington Target I meet all kinds of people from other countries. They come to visit the famous Mall of America. I work in the fitting room where they try on clothes that are actually cheaper here than in their own country. I talk to them and learn where they are from, and when I get home, I look up their country to learn about it.

I feel strongly that it is God's wish that I understand the people of His world. I don't know exactly why; I just have full joy in doing it.

Helen Manar was born in Murray, Utah, and is the daughter of Bert and Thelma Brown. She attended Westminster College in Utah and moved to Minnesota in 1961. She loves reading and enjoys getting to know people. Helen and her daughter, Jennie, who lives with her, share a love for animals of all kinds. Together they care for six birds, five guinea pigs, two ferrets, one rabbit, nine hamsters, several fish in two tanks, and one spoiled cat. Helen has two children and two grandchildren. Her nephew Bert Goff also makes his home with Helen and calls her Mom.

Wherefore, I, Lehi, prophesy according to the workings of the Spirit which is in me, that there shall none come into this land save they shall be brought by the hand of the Lord.
2 Nephi 1:6

"As a hen gathereth her chickens..."

BY CHER JENSEN

THE HEAVENS HAVE ALWAYS BEEN a source of answers for me. The scriptures tell of the star that appeared in the sky as a sign of the Savior's birth. The rainbow was given as a sign from the heavens of a covenant made by the Lord with His people. As a child I pictured Christ looking upward to His Father in heaven as He prayed. I knew He had to be a separate personage, and this led me to the discovery of the true Church.

In my teen years I prayed that I might be given belief and faith in God. I found my answer as I looked toward the stars and saw the immensity of space and the eternities. I knew there had to be a God to create all that.

In later years I began to feel unimportant and unloved. Again I searched the heavens. It is this experience I would like to share.

I was on the roof deck of my apartment building in Minneapolis. As I looked upward at the skies, I began to feel once again the immensity of all creation. I thought again of God and how He promised that He would care for all creatures, both large and small. Even though I was but a small particle of this great world, I prayed that I might feel His loving hand in my life.

Just then the caretaker came up and called for me to help. Someone had let a Bantam chicken loose in the hallway. The poor creature was terrified and was flapping her wings all about. I told the caretaker to get a paper bag in which I was able to capture the chicken. I then transferred it to a box. Later that evening I called a friend to drive me to the zoo. As it was after hours, I had to climb over the fence with the chicken so I could put it in an enclosed area with other birds. (A few years later I was reminded of this incident when I visited the Honolulu Zoo and saw a similar Bantam chicken.)

I was grateful that the Lord showed me that He did love all creatures, including me, and that He allowed me to be in His service to rescue one of those creatures. I continue to look toward the heavens as I await the Savior's coming.

THE TITLE OF THIS STORY IS QUOTED FROM 3 NEPHI 10:4.

Cheryl ("Cher") Jensen was born in Brainerd, Minnesota. She was baptized in the Bryant Avenue chapel in Minneapolis in 1959. She holds a bachelor's degree in elementary education and loves children and art. Retired now after thirty-seven years in the telecommunications industry, she continues her extensive genealogical research and serves as a family history consultant. Cher is known for lovingly reaching out to people around her. Her parents were Elmer Jensen and Margaret Westphal.

A Daughter of
My Heavenly Father

BY SHEKINAH VILLANUEVA

On New Year's Day of 2012, I got my appendix taken out. It wasn't a major surgery, and I knew that appendicitis was quite common, but I was still pretty nervous. When my dad came to visit me, he took my hand and said, "You are a child of God." I guess I have always been taught that, but it took me a while to know it for myself. That day I felt my Heavenly Father's hand in mine, just like my earthly father's, and I felt like a true daughter of God.

Months later I had the opportunity to go to Especially For Youth, a week-long church-sponsored camp. There it was etched onto my brain that because my Heavenly Father, the King of the universe, is my literal spiritual Father, being his daughter means that I'm capable of doing hard things. Thinking of Him as my actual dad for the first time made me more sensitive towards the good things around me and more thankful for the Atonement that makes it possible for me to come back to Him.

I am a daughter of my Heavenly Father, who loves me and I love Him. Knowing that I am His daughter gives me strength to know that He will never abandon me and that He will never give me more than I can handle. This confidence is something I want for everyone around me. If everybody knew the divine potential within them because of their heavenly lineage, we would all have the courage to fight for right, and it would be a lot easier to choose the right.

Shekinah Villanueva was born in Quezon City, Philippines, and moved with her family to the United States and the Apple Valley Ward in June 2007. Her parents are Elmer and Abegail Villanueva. In high school she participated in track and field events and choir. She also did volunteer work with the National Honor Society. Shekinah will enter BYU-Provo in September 2013. She enjoys traveling, eating, playing the piano, hanging out with her family, and going into the Twin Cities with her friends. She is looking forward to serving a mission.

His Enveloping Love

BY L. NOËL HOSMAN

NOW AS I REFLECT ON THE TIMES that the Lord has touched me spiritually, I am drawn to my last experience in the temple before leaving for the mission field.

It was the end of our last week in the Language Training Mission, and our district had the opportunity to attend an evening endowment session one last time. Unlike other sessions, however, this one would be live and in our mission language. It was exciting and fatiguing as four hours slipped by. Afterwards, I found myself back in the temple waiting room staring at the exit door, holding tightly to a railing and sobbing so hard that my whole body shuddered. At first I didn't know what was going on. It was as if I was watching someone else experiencing this, and I didn't know how to relate. But when the first sob slipped from my throat followed by many other soft uncontainable sobs, I realized this was me, and my face and hands were already wet from my streaming tears.

As a crowd formed around me, I wanted to know what was going on and why, but I was unable to speak. In my heart I was asking this same question of my Heavenly Father when clarity came and I realized that we are made up of two parts, one physical and one spiritual. At that very moment in time my spiritual side realized that it would be another sixteen months before I would be able to return again to a temple and feel wrapped in my Heavenly Father's love, and that was unbearable.

When I returned from my mission sixteen months later, I met my parents in the Los Angeles Temple where we were able to be together again. Once more I felt washed in Heavenly Father's love and the love of my earthly parents as well.

Linda "Noël" Hosman was born in Anchorage, Alaska, the daughter of Herbert Allan Hauser and Sidna Ednale Folk. Her mother was converted to the Church when Noël was 2 years old, and her father joined when she was 11. She became a licensed beautician after high school and was the first in her family to serve a mission (Japan) and to graduate from BYU, where she met her "Sweetie." They moved to Apple Valley, Minnesota, on Thanksgiving Day 1988 to live near family. Noël and Tom have shared this journey called life with five children who have become wonderful men. Noël has been interested in just about everything at one time or the other.

Sunset Messages

BY JESSICA FRIEDMAN

I HAVE OFTEN MARVELED at the beauty of a sunset. I've watched the sunset in far off places, on mountaintops, over the ocean, and right in my backyard. No matter where I am, I always have the same feeling. I feel God's love for me.

After my freshman year of college, I went home to Southern California, and I fell into a deep depression. Often I would drive to the beach, and I would sit on the sand and weep for hours. Not only was I sad, I felt immense guilt for being sad. I felt like I was wasting the precious gift of life. The guilt for not feeling happy was almost worse than not being happy. Or perhaps it was just a vicious cycle. I would sit on that beach and wait for the sunset to come. The beach was always quiet by the evening, and often I would be alone watching the sun fall into the ocean and seeing the brilliant colors dance across the sky. It was in these moments that God showed me His majesty. The sunset could speak to my soul. It was a secret message just for me and just for a moment.

I knew God was sending His love to me. He knew my pain. He knew my guilt. And in those sunsets, I knew He loved me no matter what.

Now as a young mother, I often sit by my back door at the end of the day and watch the sun set over the ballpark. Every time I watch this marvelous work of God, I feel a message just for me. A message of God's love. I can feel Him saying, "Good job today. You are my daughter and I love you."

Jessica Friedman graduated from BYU with a B.S. in computer science. She is currently working as a stay-at-home mom, caring for her husband, Dan, and their three children. Jessica was born in Boise, Idaho, and is the daughter of Mark and Annette Bowler. She and her family moved to Minnesota in 2012. Jessica enjoys swimming and going on nature walks.

A Daughter of God

BY MARISSA STOTTS

I JUST FELT LIKE I NEEDED TO SHARE AN EXPERIENCE I had at Young Women Encampment last summer. It was the last day, which meant it was testimony meeting day. My friend told a story about something that happened earlier in the week. She said she was sitting in her room with her roommate. She must have been really depressed that day because she just came out and said, "I'm so ugly. I'm so ugly."

Her roommate was surprised about this because this young woman was very active, funny, nice, and most definitely not ugly. So her roommate said exactly what she thought and what she knew was true: "No, you are not. You are a beautiful daughter of God."

From this I learned that it doesn't matter if you're not popular, or that your clothes aren't up-to-date, or you don't wear makeup. You are still a beautiful daughter of God.

Marissa Stotts will enter eighth grade at Falcon Ridge Middle School in September. She was born in Oregon City, Oregon, to Kelly and Maria Stotts, and at age five moved to The Netherlands. Two years later she moved to Apple Valley, Minnesota. She enjoys drawing, playing the piano and French horn, and singing. She also loves soccer, especially when she can play goalie.

And never could be a people more blessed than were they, and more prospered by the hand of the Lord. And they were in a land that was choice above all lands, for the Lord had spoken it.
Ether 10:28

My Testimony Rests on God's Love

BY HEATHER LEAVITT

WHEN I WAS A YOUTH, the stake challenged us to prepare names from our own family history and do the temple work for them. Both of my parents joined the church as teenagers, so there is lots of work to be done in my family.

I remember my mom and me working together in the family history library as we researched names. The Holy Ghost is quick to confirm the importance of family history work, and we felt it intensely as we worked together in the library. We compiled a list, and I was very excited because one of the people I was going to be baptized for was a girl named Ada, who died when she was around my same age. I knew nothing about her really, but I felt that we had a connection because of our similar ages.

The process was that we had to download our names to a floppy disk and take it to the temple. The staff at the family history center helped us, but when we took the disk to the temple to get everything ready before the day we were to do the baptisms, there was nothing on the disk. The first time it happened, it felt like it was just a computer glitch, but the second time it happened, it started to feel like opposition, and that confirmed to us that we must be doing something important. The third try was the charm, and we were able to go to the temple as a family and complete the work.

Computer problem or not, this experience really strengthened my testimony of family history work and also let me feel the love Heavenly Father has for every one of us. He loves his children so much that He has given us the opportunity to help our family get blessings they never received in this life. My testimony rests completely on the love I have felt personally from my Heavenly Father. The fact that I am a daughter of God and He loves me has kept me afloat through many times where I felt afraid, anxious, and alone. When I view the gospel from the perspective of Heavenly Father's love for us, my testimony and my faith grow. I love this Church and the peace I have access to when I follow Heavenly Father's teachings.

Heather Leavitt moved to Minnesota in March 2012. She was born in Riverside, California, but grew up in Nampa, Idaho. Her parents are Doug and Brenda Campbell. A member of the Church all her life, Heather loves playing the organ. She studied political science at Boise State University, worked for a time in accounts receivable, and is currently a stay-at-home mom. She and her husband, Adam, have two children, and she loves keeping a journal about the children. She also likes trying new recipes.

Moments
of Stillness

BY MELISSA JEANNE NIELSEN

FIVE FORTY-FIVE A.M. I am sitting on my couch, meditating. I've been up for an hour already, partially due to the 4:45 wake up of the baby, but mostly because in a few minutes, I will be leaving to go to the temple.

A door creaks. It's the girls' door. Little feet trod out, still sleepy with every step. This is my Elaine, clad in pink princess pjs, blond bed head hair, and a binky hanging out of her mouth.

She sees me, rubs her eyes and climbs up on my lap. "Ginky!" She says as she thrusts her second binky at me. She wraps my arms around her and snuggles in. Together we watch the sun rise on the second spring morning after a long, difficult winter.

As her pudgy fingers interlace with mine, I sigh. I pull her a little tighter, and my mind starts the thought, "So much for meditation." As quickly as the thought started, it was replaced with something else.

"Be still, and know that I am God."

I know my God, my Heavenly Father and Heavenly Mother, through my children. My goal as a parent is not to teach them who God is, but to not destroy the innate knowledge that was pre-programmed in them when they came.

And as I struggle to teach them how to live here, how to overcome their challenges, and meet their divine potential as children of Heavenly Parents, I see glimpses that they know more than I do. When we do talk about God, we do not tell them that they must be good because God will be sad if they aren't. We do not talk of the hellfire and damnation that is so often used as a scare tactic. Rather, we stress the love. We talk about God as a Person who wants us to be happy, who has shown us a way to be happy and, ultimately, share that happiness with Him.

Lady Elaine only has two years on my thirty. She hasn't been removed from God for nearly as long as I have. She is closer than I am. And so, I do not sit down to inform my children of God or of spirituality. Instead, I take those moments as the sun is rising to be still as my children remind me of what I once knew and understood.

Melissa Jeanne Nielsen submitted this essay to Kveller.com for their short essay contest on talking to your children about God. She was one of fourteen women selected in the Twin Cities to read an essay about motherhood in the 2013 "Listen to Your Mother" program. Melissa was born in Grand Rapids, Michigan, but has lived in Minnesota since age 2 (excepting her college years) so she claims Minnesota as her native land. Her parents are Reo and Merle Burnham Pratt. She has a bachelor's degree in music education from BYU-Provo and uses her talents to collaborate with her husband, Matt, in composing and arranging music, often on contract from the Church. She has four children, a trampoline, and a blog. She also points out that she can do the splits.

That they may see, and know, and consider, and understand together, that the hand of the Lord hath done this, and the Holy One of Israel hath created it.
Isaiah 41:20

*And in nothing doth man offend God, or against none is his wrath
kindled, save those who confess not his hand in all things
and obey not his commandments.*
Doctrine & Covenants 59:21

Gaining Strength from the People We Love

An Example of
Strength and Courage

BY BROOKLYN GARDNER

MY THIRD-GREAT-GRANDMOTHER Margaret Miller Watson DeWitt was born in Glasgow, Scotland, on January 16, 1841. Her mother died when she was only 12, and she and her sister sold the house and moved into a small apartment.

She soon discovered the Church and would secretly go to church meetings without her sister knowing. When her sister found out, she whipped her, telling her that she was forbidden from meeting with the missionaries.

Over the next couple of years Maggie worked in a textile mill. By the age of 14 she had the ability to work ten looms at a time. This skill was highly unusual for a girl of her age. It was also very dangerous as her skirts or body parts could easily become entangled in the looms and take her life. However, she took the risk to earn the money she needed to join the Saints in America and get baptized. She hid the extra money from her work in her shoes.

Her sister resorted to tying Maggie down to the bed when she was not working to keep her from going to the Mormon meetings. Finally the day arrived. Margaret left after breakfast early in the morning taking only the clothes on her back and a nightcap. She went directly to her Mormon friends, the McKays, and they hid her for two weeks until the next ship to America arrived. The McKay family she stayed with turned out to be President David O. McKay's grandparents. She traveled by ship for six weeks and landed in New York at the age of 15. She was soon baptized and made the long journey west to Utah.

I've always liked stories about my ancestors, and I think Margaret's story is touching. It hits on a personal level for me. She was so strong. Sometimes I see friends who are interested in the Church, but they start having trouble because their families don't want them to join. I often tell them this story, and it helps both them and me.

Brooklyn Gardner is the oldest child in a family of five. Her parents are Joel and Shantel Gardner. She was born in Chandler, Arizona, and moved to Minnesota in 2008. In the fall she will be a junior at Apple Valley High School. She enjoys history and art, especially drawing.

My Last Trip with Mom

BY KRISTINE MILLER

I WAS VERY MUCH LOOKING FORWARD TO MY TRIP to Hawaii in May 2008. My daughter Tara and her husband Chris married in April, but postponed their reception until May for several reasons. Also, my mother, my younger sister Kim, my niece Michelle and her husband Joey and their two boys live in Hawaii, and I was anxious to see them. Kim had been Mom's caregiver for several years, and since I was coming for the reception, I could spend time with Mom and give Kim a break.

Each time I had been reunited with Mom I noticed the change in her strength, appearance, and abilities. She was becoming progressively weaker and sleeping more and more. She always needed her walker now, and her steps were slow and cautious. Mornings, following a small breakfast, she would nap until nearly noon. Afternoons we would sit on her balcony and talk. She was often confused and would repeat many of the same questions. One day she said, "I think I'm 83. Is that right?" I said, "No, Mom, you were born October 3, 1916. On your birthday you'll be 92." She opened her mouth and got an astounded look on her face, as if it just couldn't be true. I told her I could hardly believe it myself. Then I recited the names and ages of each of her children and grandchildren. Again, the look of surprise. I remember when she was sharp as a tack, and when her hair was brown, and she could walk quickly and hear well. It certainly didn't seem to be more than fifty years since Mom was relatively young.

One day Kim asked me to bring Mom on the handy van to Mililani, where Kim teaches at the high school. This minibus circles the island of Oahu, picking up and dropping off passengers along the way. Kim said, "Be sure to bring Honeybee [her dog]. Otherwise she will stand at the window and bark and cry until we return. The bus driver knows Honeybee, and it's okay." So I put that little mutt in a large open purse and we three waited on the bench outside the apartment for the late bus. Although the bus was cooler than outside, it still wasn't comfortably cool, and the seats were hard. I noticed an elderly man looking at us, and then he leaped toward me and fastened my seat belt, pulling the strap much too tight. "Good grief," I thought. "Next time I come to Hawaii, I'll rent a car!"

As we traveled, we picked up and dropped off passengers. I noticed both the beauty and the poverty of that part of Honolulu. Eventually we made it onto the highway, just in time for the afternoon traffic jam. But I enjoyed the scenery. The koa trees and palm trees, the greenery on the mountains, and a pineapple plantation. We were finally making progress, but then left the highway and climbed a high winding hill. A young man sitting two rows in front of us put on his backpack and grabbed his white cane. A middle-aged woman was standing on the corner and smiled as the

My three daughters and I were together in Hawaii for the wedding reception. This was just before Tamari left on her mission. We are (left to right) Tiffany, Maria, me, and Tamari.

bus approached. I wondered why she looked so happy because the bus must have been very late. This young man must have been her son. She smiled brightly, then put her arm in his as they walked to their house, he using his white cane in front of him.

When we finally arrived, I wasn't in a really cheerful mood but was happy to get off the bus. Kim changed Mom into her swimsuit, and we watched as she swam a little, but mostly floated. Her osteoporosis had robbed her of her strength to swim lengths, but this activity was something she really looked forward to.

Chris and Tara's wedding reception was in Ko'olina at the Marriott. There were four lagoons near the hotel, and beyond each lagoon is the magnificent Pacific Ocean. I was astounded by the beauty of this part of the island.

The following year was mostly difficult for Mom as she weakened even more and eventually lost her appetite altogether. On

November 9, 2009, just after her shower, Kim wrapped her in a blanket, brought her to bed, and was drying her body when Mom slipped away, as in the twinkling of an eye and in perfect peace.

The last time Mom and I traveled together was on that old bus to Mililani. I remember all that I saw that day, especially the young blind student and his mother and her happy smile as she greeted him. I would have missed that experience if I had rented a car and driven in comfort.

So many times since then I've expressed gratitude in my prayers for eyes that see and for all my experiences.

Kristine Miller enjoys reading, swimming, and playing the piano. Her favorite activity, however, is spending time with her grandchildren. She was born in Houston, Texas, moved to Minneapolis and then, at the age of 28, moved to Apple Valley. Her parents were Maurits Karlson and Eleanor Storland. Her mother joined the Church in 1952, so Kristine was raised in the Church. She has five children and nine grandchildren.

Alice

BY LISA JANE YOUNG

THE PHONE CALL CAME around 8:40 a.m. It was my mum crying and telling me that my gran had suffered a stroke and was in a coma and would probably lose seventy percent of her brain function if she recovered. The doctors said that they could see her living only a couple more days. I was devastated. This was the part I hated about living so far from home and my family, not being able to jump in the car to support them. I explained that I would try to fly home to England. As usual, my mum did not want to trouble me, but I was insistent that I would do everything in my power to get home. At the time my husband was working for the airline, and there was a possibility that I could fly standby.

I arrived in Manchester early Wednesday morning and went straight to the hospital. I will never forget seeing my grandma in a coma with a breathing mask on, looking so small and frail.

My mum and dad left me alone with her and I told her I was there and how much I loved her. I said, "Nana, I am having

Lisa Young shares a big hug with her grandmother Alice and two of her sons, Matthew and Louis, in January 2012

a baby and, if I have a girl, I will name her Alice after you." I was six weeks pregnant.

Over the next couple of days I spent time with her, holding her hand, singing hymns, and reading. I found it interesting that the lesson being taught at church the next week was regarding death and how life is not over when death calls but that the spirit lives on. I read this lesson to her on Thursday afternoon. I read from the Book of Mormon in Third Nephi when Jesus visits the Nephites and teaches them his gospel. As I read, I distinctly remember the feeling of darkness being vacuumed out of the room and being replaced with light and peace. I knew that the Spirit was with us.

That night in the hospital I could not help but chuckle to myself. I was sat by her bedside and mum was on the other side. In unison, my gran and mother snored and looked so much alike.

Lisa Jane Young: "Alice"

Alice Young was named for her great-grandmother, fulfilling the promise Lisa made.

I had always avoided death before, but this time I knew I needed to hold its hand and force myself to understand how loved ones will inevitably leave this world.

We went home to shower the next morning. When we arrived back at the hospital, the doctor's face said it all. My dad and two brothers were sat with her. We entered the room, and I watched as she took her final breath. I felt numb, but I stood and kissed her face a couple of times. "It's okay, Gran. I'll be in the temple for you next year," I promised.

It was my first genuine encounter with the passing of someone I loved dearly, but the memories I have of spending three precious days with her I will forever cherish in my heart. That was the most time I had spent with her in my whole life at one given time. I believe that she knew me and my mum were there and she felt the love we had for her.

Tuesday, November 27, at 12:03 a.m. my beautiful baby girl entered the world, and my mum was able to be with me to witness the arrival of baby Alice.

My knowledge of the plan of salvation eases the pains of my gran's passing, and I know that she is in a much better place, where worldly things are no longer important and where she too will have the opportunity to learn the true gospel of Jesus Christ.

Lisa Jane Young was born in Manchester, England, the daughter of Michael Joseph and Carol Belhomme. She moved to the United States in 2001 and became an American citizen in 2012. She is trained in the culinary arts, graduating six days before her first child was born. She and her husband, Mark, joined the Church in 2006. They have three sons and a daughter. Lisa would love to find more time to read and paint.

Remaining Faithful

BY TRINA MALLER

THE MISSIONARIES coming to the house influenced me to join the Church. I was living in Bloomington [Minnesota] then and my children were at home. But it was the warmth of the people that I loved the most. I had never really been happy in my former church.

My son thinks I should get more involved in church now. "Go, if you've got the chance," he tells me. But I can't get out much. I like it when members of the Church stop by to visit me, my home teachers and visiting teachers, I mean.

And I really do love going to the "Ladies Who Lunch" potluck every month. I like to listen to the sisters talk about things. I always feel a little embarrassed because I don't talk much—I can't think of anything to say—but I love to hear what they say, and the food is always so good. I appreciate the sisters who give me rides.

Trina Maller lives in Ecumen Centennial House, an assisted living center in Apple Valley. She is under a doctor's care for progressive dementia. She was born in Milwaukee, Wisconsin, and attended grade school there. When her father, James Sparakis, passed away, her mother, Ione, moved the family to Minneapolis. Trina met her husband when they were in high school, but she went on to business school and worked as a secretary in a doctor's office before they were married and until her children came. She has two children and six grandchildren. Her friends at church admire her positive outlook and gentle nature.

HER SON, BRAD, RECALLS that when he was growing up his mother was always friendly and concerned about others. When he had friends over, she was warm and inviting and usually offered the boys a treat or other food. He admits that she was too trusting and he got away with a lot as a teen. He also says that his mother enjoyed reading, liked to eat out, and was often involved with a church.

My Grandfather's Love

BY MELISSA JEANNE NIELSEN

DURING THE LAST YEAR of Matt's undergraduate work at BYU, we were living in a rundown apartment, barely squeezing by. Brody was almost two, Charlotte was not quite a year old, and even in our student ward, we were considered poor.

At that time we lived about twenty minutes away from my grandfather. My grandmother had passed away the year prior, and he was living on his own. He offered to help us out with food costs if we would make him dinner three times a week. We took him up on this offer, primarily to spend time with him and have our children around him as much as possible, but the help with food was very welcome. He was almost 90 years old at the time. We knew we would be leaving Utah soon, and that time with him was limited.

We spent a lot of time out in Salem, Utah. We picked walnuts with him in his backyard. We enjoyed many meals with him, listening to his stories and watching his eyes light up as he held

Charlotte on his lap. I would often bring my French horn with me to play for him. He was a very skilled musician. We would play duets on piano and flute. We would listen to Mozart together. He told me about playing trumpet in the first Oakland Temple Pageant. He was bored with the parts and decided that he would sneak up into the balcony and play the fanfares from there. The conductor was less than pleased with him, but it started a tradition that carried through until the pageant was discontinued in 2007.

Over the months his memory started to leave him. He would often call me by the name of one of his sisters or his daughters. I often had to reintroduce him to Matt, to which he would respond, "Well, I knew who Matt Nielsen is, but I didn't know he was married to my granddaughter! That's amazing!"

One particular evening when we came, he was sorting through an extensive coin collection. He began to tell us about the more rare coins, and then he picked up a tiny silver heart. "You've never seen a coin like that, I bet." I shook my head, and he told me another story:

It was WWII. He wasn't eligible for military duty, so he worked as a photographer for the local newspaper. At that time photographers developed their own film, so he spent many hours in a darkroom. (As an aside, I remember him teaching me how to develop film in a darkroom in our basement when I was growing up. It is something that I loved to do, and even though the days of film are long gone, I will always yearn for the opportunity to do it again.) At the end of each day, he would take the silver filaments from the developing solution and collect them in a small film canister. Finally, after five or six years of collecting, he had

Above, Grandpa Nephi Hurley Pratt and Charlotte Metta Nielsen at Charlotte's baby blessing, September 2008.
Left, the silver heart my grandfather made for my grandmother as an anniversary present.

filled that canister. He formed a small mold of a heart and melted down that silver. That was the gift that he gave my grandmother for their anniversary that year.

We learned a lot from Grandpa. Most nights we played Scrabble. We pulled the Scrabble tiles out of an old cookie jar that lived on top of a tattered Scrabble dictionary. We used letter stands that he had carved himself. One night, he scored ninety points by putting down the letter "J." I never did beat him. The man read the dictionary when he was bored. It wasn't possible to beat him (although I think my sister may have won one night when he was sick). I did learn that you can almost always play the word "JO" if you can't get rid of a pesky "J" and that "QAID" is one of the only "Q" words that doesn't need a "U."

The day after Christmas I received word that he had been admitted to the hospital in Provo. At 7 a.m. I ran outside, scraping the snow and ice off our car. I met my sister at the hospital. It wasn't the first time he had been admitted, but it was different this time.

As we visited with Grandpa, we found him to be in good spirits. We brought Christmas treats with us, and we enjoyed them together. We left after a while so that the nurses could help him bathe. My sister pointed out that there was a DNR sticker on his chart. We knew that we might have only a few days. I made the call to my father and told him it was time to come out. It was one of the hardest phone calls I've ever made.

The next few days were sacred. At one point the doctor asked him if he had any questions. My grandpa looked at him and asked, "Do you sing in your ward choir?" The doctor looked him in the eye and said, "Why yes, I do." Grandpa said, "Good. I can trust a man who sings in his ward choir."

I remember my dad's cell phone ringing about 1:30 a.m. It had happened. My grandfather had just passed a few minutes earlier. I handed my dad the keys to my car. I couldn't go back to sleep. After lying there for a while, a voice told me to go clean my kitchen. I ignored it. Again, I was encouraged to go clean my kitchen. So I did. We didn't have a dishwasher, and the dishes had piled up over the last few days. So I started washing dishes. When I finished the dishes, I started to go back to bed. This time, that voice in my head told me to go mop my floor. At this point it was 3:30 in the morning. I listened. As I was on my hands and knees mopping my kitchen floor, the tears were finally able to flow freely. I was able to mourn. It was a very private experience, which is how I prefer my mourning to be. I hate crying in public. Around 4 a.m. I went back to bed. Matt and the kids slept through the whole thing.

That day was Saturday, January 3, 2009. The next day was Brody's birthday. We had planned a little celebration that morning. I had debated about canceling it, but when my dad arrived home from the hospital, we all felt that it would be best to have some sort of distraction. As we were leaving to go to the party, I saw the note tacked to my door about the carpet cleaning that day. All of our living room furniture needed to be moved into the kitchen to facilitate the cleaning. Because I had cleaned the kitchen earlier that morning, we were able to move everything easily and quickly. Had I not cleaned my kitchen that morning, we would've had some extra stress heaped on us as we quickly attempted to pull it together. We didn't need it that day—we couldn't handle it that day.

At Grandpa's funeral a few days later, Emma and I played the arrangement of "When He Comes Again" that Grandpa often practiced. My grandfather often testified of the love that the Savior has for us and of the power of the Atonement. This song represents to me his final testimony to his progeny. He indeed exemplified the lyrics of the song:

Each day I'll try to do his will
And let my light so shine
That others seeing me may seek
For greater light divine.

It is a simple thing. It may sound silly to say that the Holy Ghost told me to clean my kitchen. But I know that our Heavenly Father works in diverse ways. What I needed that morning was a clean kitchen and an opportunity to sort through emotions. I needed to grieve. Many times since, I've seen how the hand of the Lord works this way in my life. Most often, it is in little things that many people would say God doesn't care about.

In the years since, I've seen my fair share of struggles. I've doubted and I've questioned teachings. In the end, no matter the issue that I may be grappling with, I can't deny that I have Heavenly Parents who love me and are aware of my joys and my struggles. Christ did atone for me, not just for my sins, but for the times when I hurt. I think that all of us forget that second part, and I think that all of us tend to need that second part more than we think. The Atonement is real, and it is for each of us individually.

Melissa Jeanne Nielsen was born in Grand Rapids, Michigan, to Reo and Merle Burnham Pratt, but has lived in Minnesota since age 2 (excepting her college years) so she claims Minnesota as her native land. She has a bachelor's degree in music education from BYU-Provo and uses her talents to collaborate with her husband, Matt, in composing and arranging music, often on contract from the Church. She has four children, a trampoline, and a blog. She also points out that she can do the splits.

Max

BY MARIA STOTTS

WHEN I WAS A LITTLE GIRL, we had an older gentleman in our ward named Max. He was like an adopted grandpa to the kids. I especially loved to sit on his lap during church, and he would always have a candy in his pocket for me. He called me "Peaches," and I could never walk by him without receiving a hug. As I grew up, Max still called me Peaches, and I still gave him hugs. I eventually moved away, got married, and settled with my little family about two hours away from my hometown.

One day I attended the temple, and when I got to the part of the session where I was presented at the veil, I heard a very familiar voice that filled me with love and happiness. I couldn't place it. At first I thought it was someone who sounded like a General Authority, but after a little bit, I recognized it as Max! I knew that there was someone on the other side of the veil who loved me and was waiting for a hug. It was a joyful reunion, but more than anything, I was reminded that there really is a loving Friend waiting for us who loves us and can't wait to give us a hug.

Maria Stotts enjoys music, singing, reading good books, dancing, exercising, and traveling. Born in Springfield, Oregon, she was raised in the Church and met her husband, Kelly, at BYU, where she received a degree in family sciences in 1993. She has been working as a mother ever since. Her family moved to Minnesota in 2007 and for the past four years she has served as a seminary teacher. She is the daughter of Melvin L. Westover and Marilyn R. Wartena.

Grandma and Grandpa

IN MEMORIAM
ROBERT A. CROW
JULY 4, 1930 – APRIL 20, 1995
GISELA T. CROW
APRIL 5, 1922 – APRIL 20, 1995

BY LONI DAVIS

IT WAS SPRING 1995, my junior year of college at BYU. I was busy preparing for finals, packing up for the summer, and getting ready to leave on a two-month, study-abroad trip to Namibia, Africa. And now I had to attend a funeral.

The phone call came in the middle of the night. My roommate came into my room and woke me up. My mom and dad struggled on the other line as they told me they had just gotten a call from the Iowa state troopers confirming the death of my grandma and grandpa. They had been traveling up from their home in Illinois to visit their first great-grandson, my nephew, who had been born a few months before, and to see my parents in Minnesota. They had stopped in Marshalltown, Iowa, to see a train-set exhibit, when upon leaving the parking lot, a semitruck T-boned them. The man driving the truck was speeding and high on drugs. My grandmother died instantly, and it was reported that as my grandfather was being lifted up onto the stretcher, his last words were, "I'm broken."

A piece of me broke that day as well. I had never in my life received such tragic news. I fell to the ground and cried and cried. My roommates tried to comfort me, but the shock and the pain were overwhelming.

My grandpa had been a safety inspector for the railroads. Even after retirement he still had a passion for trains and train sets. As a hobby he loved making electric train sets from scratch in his basement. They were elaborate sets made up of little towns with people, bridges, houses, schools, mini stop-lights, fire stations, and other such buildings. The little towns would lead to rolling countryside, hills, and farmland. I looked forward every vacation to seeing what his new train set would look like. I would spend hours down there in his basement with him, running the trains forward and backward and moving the little people and trees around.

My grandma had hobbies too that she tried sharing with me. One time she took me golfing. First, she taught me how to hold the golf clubs correctly and hit the golf ball in their huge front yard. Then she took me to the golf course and patiently waited as I sank ball after ball into the water. I was determined to be as good a golfer as she was. After many lost balls, we both decided this was not the hobby for me. Still, she said I did great, even though I knew I did not; but she made me feel like I did. Not wanting to

My family and I visited my grandpa and grandma in 1994. This is the photo I carried with me to Africa after their death.

lose any more golf balls in the water, she decided to take me bowling. My grandma was on a bowling league, and this was a much better fit for me. At least when I got a gutter ball, the ball would come back to me unlike the golf balls. We enjoyed going bowling together many times after that.

Grandma and Grandpa lived in a small town and did not get out of it too often. They were rightfully nervous when I told them that I was going to go on a two-month, study-abroad trip to Namibia, Africa. But instead of making me feel bad and expressing their feelings openly, my grandma sent me some money for the trip and wrote me a letter saying, "Have a nice, safe, pleasant trip to Africa. Yes, I think that's nice that you can go. I've thought that would be a nice place to go. But I'm a nut on wildlife films. Sending a few dollars to help you out on [your] trip. Take care. Love Grandma."

Just two months after I got that letter, they died, and I left for Africa a week after their funeral. I had a picture of us from the last time I had seen them in August of 1994 that I carried with me all through Africa. I carried their spirit with me as well. I felt their presence with me all through my trip and through the whole next year.

Grandma and Grandpa had been converted to The Church of Jesus Christ of Latter-day Saints by my mom who had found the Church when she was a teenager. They only stayed active in the Church for a few years. Eventually, they had their names taken off the records of the Church. I found this out while I was back at BYU for my senior year. In the spring of 1996, a year after their death, I was able to take their names to the Provo Temple and re-baptize them into the Church. I thought I was supposed to feel good about that, but as I came back to my apartment that day, I felt lonely, empty, and sad. I couldn't feel their presence with me anymore. I thought I would feel happy about the service I had performed for them. I prayed for understanding and came to realize that they weren't with me anymore, and that was a good thing. They were now busy doing heavenly work beyond the veil.

The work they were performing on the other side of the veil led me to Texas later that year. For six months I lived with my aunt Tina. My other aunt Connie lived nearby. In Tina's garage I found gravestone certificates for my grandpa's father, mother, and younger brother. I continued to research my grandfather's side of the family. I gathered lots of information from both Tina and

Connie. After months of research I found information for a few generations back on both his mother's side and his father's side of the family. I know I was being led and guided by the Spirit to be in the right places and at the right times to find this genealogy of his. I went to the Dallas temple and did their temple work before I moved back to Utah in 1997.

I still feel my grandparents' love for me even as I write this. I love them, and I am grateful for the love they have always shown for me in this life and the next.

Loni Davis is a life-long Minnesotan, having been born in St. Paul. She lived for six years in Utah while pursuing a degree in humanities at BYU-Provo. She has been a travel agent and is now a stay-at-home mom and pre-school gymnastics coach. She is also serving as Young Women's president in the Apple Valley Ward. Loni and her husband, Barton, have three daughters. Her parents are Stewart E. Peterson and Sharon A. Palmer.

Norma Storland
1922–2012

IN MEMORIAM
BY BARBARA CALISTRO

MY AUNT NORMA STORLAND was everybody's second mom! She was the example of a devoted woman who enjoyed her place as a wife, mom, and daughter-in-law in a large circle of family and friends. She worked hard, was loving, kind and smart, and was always willing to lend a hand to all she could, to anybody in need.

I have seen her, as a young mom, carry water in five-gallon pails from the lake to heat it on a small gas burner outside her home so she could wash clothes. She would gather berries in the woods to put on ice cream for all to share. She always prepared a Sunday lunch after church for all to enjoy and a Christmas meal for anyone who happened to be there. She hemmed my skirts. She taught me how to preserve tomatoes, corn, peas, and grape juice, and how to butcher chickens when time came for me to learn.

At the same time this lady was beautiful and didn't really work at it. She was funny, and she wasn't working at that either!

She was so smart and capable. After their retirement, she took up the language of Norwegian, learned to drive a car, and went on a mission with her husband.

After she became ill and had to live in a care facility, she enjoyed trips outside to smell the fresh air and see the sun and sky, the flowers and trees. She especially enjoyed trips out to lunch with her sister Marlys and me any time we could find money, time, and an excuse to go. Sometimes we would give her ice cream with a candle so she could pretend it was someone's birthday and sing "Happy Birthday." Ice cream was always her joy!

She was an example in everyone's life. Even in her death, she left everlasting memories with everybody who knew her, especially me! We all miss her very much and will always remember Norma Storland.

Barbara Calistro was born in Minneapolis, Minnesota. She is the daughter of Vern and Eleanor Storland Karlson and joined the Church as an adult. She worked in sales for thirty-five years, beginning at the old Sears store on Lake Street in Minneapolis. She has five children, seven grandchildren, and two great-grandchildren. She is pleased to say that she taught all of her grandchildren how to swim. Her greatest relaxation and enjoyment comes from performing with the Velvetones, a community choral group of mixed voices. She sings tenor.

Norma Storland

This brief biography was written by Norma's sister Marlys Lund for a "Resident of the Month" recognition at the care facility where Norma lived the last several years of her life:

"Norma was born in Madison, South Dakota, and sixteen years later moved to Baudette, Minnesota. Shortly afterwards, she went to Minneapolis where she was head girl in the downtown Bridgeman's [an ice cream store]. While she was at work one day, this handsome young sailor came in and they were instantly attracted to each other. They married and purchased a house in Eagan [which at that time was far out in the countryside surrounding the Twin Cities].

"Norma was a homemaker while her husband worked at Univac [an early computer and business machines manufacturer]. They raised four children in their lovely country home. When the children were grown and her husband was retired, they began to travel. They spent winters in Arizona, visited Norway several times, and went on many bus tours."

An additional tribute by Jacqueline A. Kellington:
The hand of the Lord was clearly evidenced by the exemplary life Norma lived. Never did she hesitate to reach out to anyone in need. Each challenge was met with a quiet confidence in the Lord. Her love for Him was apparent as she and her husband served a full-time mission in the visitor center at Temple Square. Her special love carries on in the hearts of all she served.

My Story Begins with My Grandmother

BY CHAY DOUANGPHOUXAY

I ONCE HEARD SOMEWHERE that our history doesn't begin at our birth, but it started long before then. It started with the people that came before us. My story began with my grandmother. Her life is a tragedy that I will one day write. But for the sake of time, I'll give you a brief synopsis. At the age of 5 she became an orphan. Her biological uncle and his wife took her into their care but basically made her their slave. She worked from sun up to sun down without any aid. The workload she carried was more than her tiny malnourished body could handle. It is only by the grace of God that she survived.

They would beat her and tie her to a tree in the hot scorching heat if the cattle had gotten away under her care. She wore rags, even through her teenage years. They never allowed her to go to school because that to them meant wasted time that she could be working for them instead. Even though the rest of the world would cry just imagining the torture she went through, but yet in this little woman's heart she found a way to always forgive them and still love them as though they were her parents. Even to this day, she is still ever grateful for every morsel that they fed her.

When she got old enough to marry, they sold her off to my grandfather. He was many years older than her. There is very little that any of us know about him. He died when my mom was two or three years old. My grandmother married multiple times after that. Some of her husbands died very early into her marriage, and others don't even deserve to be mentioned. She basically raised her six children, my mother and her brothers and sisters, as a single parent.

My mother's story started off on a slightly better note in that she had a great mother. My grandmother cared for my mother as much as she knew how. But the demands of survival and trying to make a living kept her away from home a lot. She sold coal for a living.

Out of necessity, my mother grew up fast. At a young age she learned to cook, clean, and care for her younger siblings as well. Due to the drama at home stemming from her stepfather, my mom had no other option but to marry my father at the age of 16. Unlike many of her peers, she was fortunate enough to make it through high school and even her first year of college prior to marrying my father.

In the midst of my birth, the country was under attack by the communists. My parents were forced to run for their lives because we were listed on the genocide list due to my grandfather's aristocratic ties to the old regime.

I was barely learning to crawl when my parents escaped across the Mekong River to find safety in the refugee camps of Thailand. Even though we lived in the refugee camps for only three years

Chay Douangphouxay: "My Story... My Grandmother"

This is one of the few photos I have from my childhood. It shows my brother and me in the refugee camp in Thailand while our family was waiting to be sponsored to the United States.

before getting sponsored to Minnesota from my father's uncle, it seemed like an eternity to endure the bitter pangs of starvation and poverty.

It sounds cliché, but coming to America gave my parents hope. It was like being lifted up and out of the hell that we were in. Life could only go up from here, right?

You could say things got a little better, but life in America came with many new challenges as well. We were strangers in a foreign land. Our relatives helped where they could but then sent us out to fend for ourselves. My parents were taken advantage of because they couldn't speak English. The sad part was that the perpetrators were some of our own relatives. Out of necessity, I was determined to learn to speak English fluently in order to stop people from taking advantage of my parents. In less than a year, I could translate at the hospital or the welfare office for my parents. I was just 4 years old.

My mother ingrained in me the importance of education and hard work. She said it was the only way I could ever alleviate my poverty and have the chance of attaining a better life. But I must never compromise my morals or values to get at it. She taught me to always do what is right and fear God. At this time, God to us was Buddha.

Fast forward to age of 9. After being separated from her mother for over ten years, my mother sponsored my grandmother to America. I had the privilege of growing up with a grandmother in the home. Shortly after, the missionaries had come to proselyte to our family. Despite being chased by Father with his gun, they continued to persevere in bringing the gospel to us. It wasn't too long until the Spirit spoke to my mother and grandmother, and they were baptized.

I didn't convert until three years later. I wanted to find out on my own that the gospel was true. As a result of a challenge from a missionary by the name of Elder John Lopez and my determination to prove that the Mormons were evil, I prayed and read the Book of Mormon in about twenty-four hours, then asked to be baptized.

There's so much more color that I still haven't painted for you in this story for two main reasons. One, there just isn't enough time because there are so many layers of complexity to my life. Second, my story is still being written. But the important elements are all here. My life alone is a miracle of God. I truly believe the Lord preserved my family so that we can be partakers of the gospel today. He chose us beginning with my grandmother, then my mother, then on to me— three very unlikely women to be an instrument in His hands. He saved us so that we can share our stories with you today.

Today I am a business professional working for a Fortune 500 company. I have an undergraduate degree in English and am pursuing my MBA in 2014. I am an award-winning author about to release my second book this coming August. I serve on the national board for Southeast Asian Americans based out of Washington D.C. I advocate for social justice and human rights. But none of these titles can compare to the title of being a member of The Church of Jesus Christ of Latter-day Saints.

I understand who I was before I came to this earth. I know of the potential of who I can become after I leave this earth. Despite the moral degradation and constant soul-searching of our society, I have a clear understanding of my purpose here in life. I know without a doubt that Joseph Smith is a prophet of God. I know the Book of Mormon is another testament of Jesus Christ written for our time. I know that Jesus is our Savior and the Son of God. I know He died on the cross for each one of us. I know after this life every loss, every heartache, every injustice will be compensated. I know we have a Heavenly Father who loves us. I know I can repent of my sins and return to live with Him again someday. Above all the sweetest promise for me is that I can live with my amazing grandmother, mother, and family forever! This is my testimony to you in the name of Jesus Christ, amen.

Chay Douangphouxay was born in Kna Kha, Laos. With her mother, Chanthavy Chanthakhoun, and her father, Somphith Douangphouxay, she came to America when she was 3 years old. She became a member of the Crystal [Minnesota] Ward when she was baptized in 1993, and she moved to the Apple Valley Ward in 2013. She has degrees in computer information systems management and English literature. She is an author, artist, and activist. She is the co-founder and co-chair of the Twin Cities Chapter of National Asian Pacific American Women's Forum (NAPAWF) and is on the board of directors for the Southeast Asian Resource Action Center (SEARAC). Chay has a delightful dog named Bailey, and she has flown a Cesna Skyhawk 172.

For I, the Lord, have put forth my hand to exert the powers of heaven; ye cannot see it now, yet a little while ... and ye shall know that I am, and that I will come and reign with my people.
Doctrine & Covenants 84:119

Hannah Hoffman
1919–2012

A TRIBUTE BY HER DAUGHTER
JACQUELYN A. KELLINGTON

HAD THE SEEDS OF NURTURING taken root in Hannah's heart long before her earthly entrance?

She was the oldest of seven children. Her mother, a nurse, spent most of her at-home time in bed suffering migraine headaches. Her father, she saw very little of. His work required much of his time in country travel. Consequently, much of the responsibility for the children fell upon Hannah's young shoulders. She loved her younger brothers and sisters. Nurturing them was easy, even natural for her, and the bond between them grew deep.

Her maternal grandmother was influential in Hannah's interest in religion. As they read together discussing Bible principles, a deep bond was created between them. While Hannah's family did not belong to any particular faith or church, her interest in religion remained. She was concerned, not only for herself and her own spiritual welfare, but also for her brothers and sisters. This concern was the motivation that moved Hannah into getting each of her brothers and sisters ready and taking them to a neighborhood church every Sunday morning.

Hannah's parents died while she was yet in her teenage years. Consequently, her responsibilities increased. The household duties as well as the care for her seven brothers and sisters fell upon her young shoulders. It was not a burden. She loved them, nurturing them was easy; it felt natural, even right.

A short time after the death of Hannah's parents, she met and married my father, John Russel Hoffman, and most naturally her brothers and sisters entered into that marriage with her. One might say it was a "package deal." It was not long before Russel's five brothers came from Wisconsin to live with them also, extending that package. It would be only seven years later when five children of their own were added to that package. The nurturing continued, even in the face of increased responsibilities. She embraced it all; she loved them all. One might imagine the busyness of that big old house on 32nd Avenue in Minneapolis. Living within its walls were a newly married couple and fourteen very active young people of all ages. In addition, Russel's parents usually came from Wisconsin to spend winters with them. True, the hours were many, and they often found Hannah exhausted. Yet, she murmured not. Again, she loved them, and the nurturing continued.

So did her interest in religion. It often nagged at her. She read the Bible often, looking for answers to some of the confusing points of doctrine, finally making it a matter of prayer. She opened her door to two young Mormon missionaries. They spoke of a prophesied Restoration, making clear those points of doctrine

Hannah Hoffman was born in Minneapolis on October 5, 1919, and graduated from high school in 1935.

that had been confusing. Her prayer had been answered. She responded by being baptized only two weeks later.

It was not long before she was called to be the Relief Society president of her ward. It was not hard for her to do what came so naturally, to nurture and care for the sisters in her charge. She loved them, all of them. Life became even busier. Her phone was never idle. It was not unusual for Hannah to sit and visit with an ill sister for great lengths of time, addressing her concerns or discussing gospel principles. It was also not unusual for her to pick up, wash, iron, and deliver laundry for a sister who was ill.

The Lord called Hannah to serve in many capacities in the stake as well as in her ward. Her favorite calling was teaching the Relief Society spiritual living lessons.

Hannah's last few years found her with Alzheimer's, a disease that robbed her of her memory. While her memory was near-

258 THE HAND OF THE LORD

ly gone, her testimony and love for the Savior remained strong. She was never hesitant in sharing that testimony and her love for the Savior with her resident friends at the care facility where she lived. Her nurturing continued. She often checked on the needs of the surrounding residents. If she recognized they were in need of assistance, she reported it to one of the aides or nurses. Often she could be found sitting by the bedside of an upset or disturbed resident, comforting them. She loved them all and was consistent in her watch.

She was loved by so many. She served so many. Her death caused the feeling of great loss. Her funeral and burial was to be in Salt Lake City.

Safe Passage

THERE WERE MANY REASONS for the strong bond that existed between Hannah and two of her great-grandsons, Bryan and Andrew Black. They wanted to attend her funeral, but because of work commitments, they were unable to leave their home in Portland in the daytime hours. They left for Salt Lake at dusk. They were both tired. Andy was driving, and the rhythm of the car soon found Bryan asleep. Andy too felt like he could doze off. His concern caused him to petition the Lord for help in staying alert that they might arrive at their great-grandmother's funeral safely. Immediately, outside his car window shone a bright light. Not as high as the stars, but clearly in his view. It was strangely different in size and shape and continued with him as he drove. A feeling of curious wonder caused Andy to drive at different speeds to see if the light would continue with him. It did. He took pictures of it.

When he stopped for gas, the light also stopped, and when Andy resumed his trip, so also did the light.

Andy and Bryan reached their destination in Salt Lake where their mother awaited their arrival. It was late, very late. Andy ran into the house, anxious to share with his mother the experience of the unusual light that had stayed with him, keeping him awake and alert all the way from Portland. He wanted her to witness it. She quickly went outside and saw the bright light, stationary in the sky, a short distance from Andy's car. Then it suddenly shot up into the heavens and out of view.

As Andy shared this experience and the pictures with me, I could not help but feel, as did others, that this was their great-grandmother Hannah, doing what she did so well, being an instrument in the Lord's hands in answer to Andrew's prayer, keeping him alert that he and his brother might arrive safely to attend her funeral. And so, the nurturing continues, even beyond the veil.

At Rest

Hannah passed away at the age of 94. Her body rests next to her husband on the foothill of the mountains in Salt Lake City.

Jacquelyn A. Kellington follows her mother's example in rendering untiring service to her family and friends. She is also devoted to the Church and frequently invites people she meets to learn more about the gospel. Jackie was born in Minneapolis, Minnesota, and joined the Church in 1963. She and her husband, Chuck, have six children.

*His purposes fail not, neither is there any who can stay his hand.
From eternity to eternity, he is the same...*
Doctrine & Covenants 76:3-4

Teaching Our Children to Love the Lord

A Letter to My Sisters

BY ANDE AMOTT

DEAR SISTERS at present and in generations to come, I have thought a lot about the admonition to write something for our Relief Society history book. While I could share many things about my life in the past, I keep feeling that I should share my life in the present. To begin to share the gospel as I have woven my tapestry thus far in my life would be impossible. I have had many experiences that have built my testimony. But I will share some thoughts that came to my mind as I looked over my journal from these past few years.

I was blessed with many trials as a youth which solidified my commitment to the gospel. How could I leave the sure foundation and a seed which I planted that brought forth such sweet fruit? At a young age I built my testimony solidly on the "rock of Christ," as alluded to in Helaman 5:12 (one of my favorites), and I testify that as the winds and storms of life have ensued, I have prevailed only with Christ as my foundation.

In my current season of life I have been blessed to be a mother. I have an 8-year-old daughter, Elizabeth, and 4-year-old son, James. I always say (a borrowed phrase) that I had to "grow my mother heart." It was not an easy transition from single sister to married sister to mother. Especially in a world that teaches women are entitled to have it all. This philosophy is an illusion and simply impossible to achieve. I have realized that when I focus outside my husband and children, I am stepping into dangerous territory. Satan is attempting to completely destroy society and he aims at the family as ordained by God. He knows that by disillusioning women he will destroy homes, communities, and generations. In a recent stake conference, our stake president, Scott Naatjes, admonished the sisters, "Turn back to your families. Use your time to prepare. Satan is destroying a generation of young men with video games and now he is after the sisters. Social media is destroying women. Don't be at ease. Turn from the social media that is distracting you. We need you! Don't spend your time doing things that just aren't important. Examine your life. Look at things you could obey and don't, and then do them, and watch as the Lord turns you into something you never could imagine. The Lord can make more out of you." This message struck me as the Spirit whispered to me that I needed to turn more of my life and time to my Heavenly Father. It inspired me to change.

I was recently asked to speak on a portion of Lehi's dream for a Relief Society event. I studied his dream and in particular the "great and spacious building." As President Boyd K. Packer stated, "Instead of looking over into the building, we are in effect living inside of it." Daily I feel the attacks from all around me

Ande and Rob Amott with their children, James and Elizabeth, attending a wedding at the Salt Lake Temple in 2011

trying to get me to let go of the iron rod I am clinging to. I must, as God directed Emma Smith in Doctrine and Covenants 25:10, "[L]ay aside the things of the world and seek for the things of a better." I must seek to take myself and my family out of the great and spacious building. I am no longer able to have one foot in the world and one foot on the strait and narrow path. For the sake of my children and family I must keep my goals riveted on guiding, teaching, and raising my children. I must place my goals on things that are everlasting. President Uchtdorf stated in a conference talk in 2010, "We need to slow down and see the things that matter most." Each day I must seek to prioritize the good, better, and best of what I need to do. I have never forgotten when Sister Julie Beck came and spoke to the women in Minnesota at the Minneapolis stake building. She taught us to list out the things we "must do, should do, would like to do" each day and remember that we only have so many hours in the day. It is of critical importance to not waste our allotted time.

My children mean everything to me. Only when I had children did I understand a small portion of God's love for us. Through motherhood I have seen how God deals with man on the earth. I am blessed to know that He loves us unconditionally and He desires for us the best. God's work is to "bring to pass the immortality and eternal life of man" and mine should be the same: to do all I can to help my children gain eternal life. As stated in scripture, "I have no greater joy than to hear that my children walk in truth" (3 John 1:4).

A woman spoke in church a few years ago and gave the example of the pioneer women, saying how their number one priority was to ensure their families made it to Zion. She said, "Do not leave your children to do other things." We must forsake many things to raise our families. The world teaches me that if I forsake these things, then I am weak. And yet, when I seek to build up the kingdom of God, I find my greatest happiness. When I am actively engaged in the rearing of my children, the relationship with my husband, and our family life together in mortality, I feel the deepest joy that I have known. I was admonished in my patriarchal blessing to remember that "raising a righteous family should be first and foremost in my life and *everything* is secondary thereunto."

I guess the message that I want to share in this book is one of my devotion and faith to the Savior and a message that my life is a continual sanctification process of trying to become a better mother, wife, and woman of God. In every season of my life my

Heavenly Father has been beside me. I want to bear testimony that I have prayed and have great faith in trying to follow the Spirit in my life each and every day. I want to be a woman prepared for the "coming of the Bridegroom" and one who is "virtuous" and has a price "far above rubies." I have a testimony of the Savior Jesus Christ and His gospel. I will keep my eyes riveted on the goal of eternal life and pray that all of us may partake of eternal life together.

Love,
Ande Amott

Ande Amott is a registered nurse with degrees from Weber State University and the University of Utah. She and her husband, Rob, moved to Minnesota in 2002, and to Rosemount in 2005. They have two children. She was born in Morgan, Utah, to Dan and Ruth Anne Heiner, and was raised in the Church. She has served in many capacities, but her favorite calling is visiting teacher. She also loves to read, jog, clean, play the piano, and go on any adventure Rob plans.

Everything You Need to Know, You Learn Ice Skating

BY MEGAN GUNYAN

BEING A MOM IS HARD WORK. I don't think I truly understood the role my mother played in my life until I had children of my own. I don't think I even understood *my* role until I saw my baby for the first time. Even then, it was a while before I needed to teach the lessons of life. At first it's just sleepless nights, constant feedings, changing diapers, and marveling at this miracle you and your husband created. Then, this cute little bundle of joy turns into a little kid who can walk, talk, ask questions, form her own opinions, read, write, and even understand things on TV. (Heaven help us!) Children become people who need guidance, direction, examples, and just *help*. This can be terrifying to a mother. Because, let's face it, if you're home with your kids all day, you are their primary example of how to react to just about anything in life. This is good and bad as it's a chance to change those things you've always wanted to change in your life and prepare your kids for those challenges you might have failed.

But, it's also tricky because they will be facing a slew of things you never had to face. How do you prepare them for a time like that?

I'll tell you how. Ice Skating.

Okay, I admit, ice skating is not the answer to all your problems, but it will help with a great many of them. Trust me on this. Here's my story:

My oldest daughter begged me to give her ice skating lessons. For years. And I always resisted because I knew it would be a challenge and I didn't want her to struggle. She is kind of small for her age, but that should make ice skating easier, right? Finally, I told her that when she turned 7 she could take ice skating lessons. So, the magic number happened, and we found some ice skates that fit her tiny feet, enrolled her in Saturday morning beginner lessons, and took off for the first practice. It was tricky. I think she thought she could just glide out there on the ice, skate around a few times, and call it good. She took one step on the ice, slid around, and fell down. Luckily, the instructors were not new to this phenomenon and had lots of volunteers handy to literally push kids to their lesson areas on the ice. My daughter did pretty well her first time. She was excited, but a bit confused. It was harder than she had anticipated. So I thought this could be a great learning opportunity, and it will teach her to never give up, that things always start out hard for the first time, but with lots of practice, she will succeed. I was pretty proud of myself for sticking in this teaching moment. She was not so impressed.

The weeks continued and she varied in her excitement each time. One time she did great and didn't fall down and wanted to skate all the way home. Another time she had troubles, fell down, and never wanted to skate again. I grew discouraged as well be-

Claire Gunyan on ice skates, showing us that perseverance and practice count in life.

cause I couldn't figure out how to give her the old attitude adjustment she needed. It seemed like her dreams of ice skating were going right down the drain. She just gave up even trying. One Saturday she came off the ice crying, and I was so frustrated we just went home. It was very discouraging.

Finally we were down to our last lesson, the last time Claire could have a positive impression of this sport that was so trying to her. I was nervous because if it went badly I knew she would never skate again. (I know my daughter.) The morning started off pretty bad. Claire had a very negative attitude even on the drive there. I grew frustrated again and, honestly, just wanted to go home. But something stopped me. Maybe it was the Spirit telling me I needed to calm down. I'm still not really sure what happened, but I think Heavenly Father knew how desperate I was to just communicate with my daughter at that moment and He gave me what I needed. Calm. Peace. Patience. All of that entered my heart at that moment and I knew what to do. Claire and I had a sincere discussion. We talked about many things, I wish I could remember every word, but it's kind of a blur. We said a little prayer. We talked about the Lord helping us through trials and struggles. I told her I loved her unconditionally and no matter what she did I would be proud of her. And I meant it. I had no idea I could be that kind of parent. The parent I had always aspired to be. The Lord literally put words into my mouth, the Spirit was there, and I knew Claire felt it.

She went on the ice. It was touch and go. If I thought miracles would happen with her skating, I was wrong. The learning still had to happen. Practice still needed to be a part of her skating career. At one point, I saw her sit down and start crying again. All I wanted to do was race out onto that ice and tell her I loved her. She slowly came back to the stands, and we had another talk. She wanted to go home, but I knew if we went home at this point she would remember her time ice skating as a quitter. It would be a bad feeling for her. I didn't want that. We sat down and talked again. I explained to her that if she went back out and skated just one time around that rink, she would feel better. She would feel success. She asked if we could say another prayer so we did. And she smiled at me, and went out and skated around that rink *twice*. But, the best part was when she came off the ice and told me how good she felt inside. And I got to tell her that was the Holy Ghost giving her a little spiritual hug. I was so proud of her. And she was so happy.

I see ice skating lessons again in our future. Because, really, everything you need to know, you can learn ice skating.

Trust me.

Megan Gunyan is an active blogger with an interest in home decor and decorative crafts. She graduated from BYU-Provo with a B.A. in public relations in 2001. She and her husband, Chad, moved to Apple Valley in 2005. They have four children. Megan was born in Athens, Ohio, to Gil Moncivais and Sheryl Griffin. She was baptized at age 8 in Idaho.

And the hand of the Lord was with them: and a great number believed, and turned unto the Lord.
Acts 11:21

My McDonald's Speech

BY FRANCES MARIE DAVIS

WHEN THE KIDS WERE GROWING UP, we had speeches about everything. We had a dating speech, for example. That way if you go out and get in trouble, you had been warned. You knew what you were doing was wrong.

When my nieces and nephews turned 12, I used to take them to McDonald's and give them my McDonald's speech. I'd show them how hard those people have to work and how they can't even afford the things you need in life, much less what you want. They don't pay them very much. So I would sit them down and explain to them that if you're smart, you can do better. It's not going to be easy. Nobody is guaranteed an easy ride. You have to work for it.

I'm not knocking people who work at McDonald's, but if you want the opportunity to have more and do more, you have to take advantage of what's there.

Kids need inspiring, but they have to know it ain't going to be easy. They need to know that people believe in them and people think they can do better. There's a whole world out there and you have to want it.

That was how my grandmother raised us and my mom raised us. Nothing was going to be easy. People just don't give you breaks, you have to earn them.

Frances Marie Davis was born in Williamston, North Carolina, the daughter of Horace and Alease Slade Davis, but she grew up in New York City. That's where, as a single parent, she raised her daughter, Cindy, and worked for the United States Postal Service for thirty-eight years. She retired to South Carolina in 2003, where she joined the Church. She moved to Minnesota in 2006 so she could help care for her grandson, David, who is "Grandma's boy."

A Quiver Full

BY DEANNA LARSON

WHEN I CAME HOME FROM MY MISSION to Venezuela in 1994, I was ready for the next order of business—marriage and family. Only, they didn't come as quickly as expected. It took me nine years to find my soul mate and be married in the temple in 2003. I was 31 and Fred was 37. But I was grateful because for several years I didn't know if I would ever have a family of my own. We were grateful to Heavenly Father for having brought us together.

Now we looked forward to having children. I came from a family of seven children, and Fred from a family of three boys. Fred used to joke that he was a family man in search of a family. Now that we had each other, we were ready to begin that family.

Only the children didn't come. After a couple of miscarriages and many tearful nights and prayers, we decided to take a medical approach to see if there was something holding us back. We prayed for our doctor to be guided to know how to help us. As we met in that visit, he suggested several things we could do to investigate our infertility. One by one, we crossed them off the list, having discovered that they were not an issue in our case. Finally, we were down to the last item, an ultrasound to check for any abnormalities in the uterus. To our great surprise, they found a very small growth—a polyp—that was causing difficulty for embryos to implant. They suggested an outpatient surgery to remove it, and as soon as that was done, we found out the next month that we were pregnant.

The children came in quick succession. For each one, we knew when it was time to allow for another spirit to join our family. Dean was born in 2006, then Josie in 2008. Lissetta joined our family in 2010, and Christine in the very beginning of 2012. The last two are only fifteen months apart.

It is interesting how our trials are viewed based on perspective. Now I can see that the two and a half years that Fred and I had together without children was really a blessing. We had courted long-distance, so it gave us a chance to be a couple and have time together, just the two of us. Now that we have four young children, it is busy and noisy in our house, and we are frequently pulled in different directions by the needs of our children. It takes effort to continue to build our husband-wife relationship. But we are grateful to have our quiver full. (See Psalm 127:5.)

Needless to say, sometimes our blessings are also our biggest challenges. For me as a mother, this is especially true. I have always had a firm testimony of the divine nature of the family as taught by God's holy prophets. But now that I am in the middle of raising a family with my husband, it is the most challenging thing I have ever done—largely because of what Heavenly Father wants my children to teach me. I am a slow learner. But I do be-

The Fred and DeAnna Larson family, 2012. Children, left to right: Christine, Josie, Lissetta, and Dean

lieve that I am progressing, however slowly, along the continuum of developing a mother heart. At least that is my hope. I know what I want to be, and yet sometimes I feel that I am so far away from my goal. But I keep pressing forward with faith that this is the path He wants me to be on, and that some day, with faith and diligence and hope as Alma teaches in the parable of the seed, I can become what I desire to be.

I have felt the hand of the Lord guiding me along the way. Many times this has come as I have reflected on how a particular situation with my children was handled. The Spirit helps put into my mind a better way that I could have responded, showing me what it looks and feels like. Then, when the situation happens again, I can hopefully respond in a better way. There have been times when I have handled a situation in a desirable way, and I

Doing what's most important—taking time with my girls.

look back and realize it was the Spirit helping me to do what I have been shown in past reflections. Then I am sure to acknowledge His help by offering a quick heartfelt prayer of thanks.

My children are also teaching me more about repentance and hope. At one point, I was very frustrated because I couldn't seem to overcome a particular thorn in my mothering side. I sincerely repented, again and again. In meeting with a wise priesthood leader, I tearfully asked him, "How many times can I repent for the same thing? I feel like I'm failing." To which he responded that we don't fail until we quit trying. Hope is something I hang on to, giving me the ability to keep moving forward. I know I am a very imperfect mother, but I have faith, and I have hope, and I will keep moving forward. And my children have access to the same Atonement that I have access to, and it will fill in the cracks from my inadequacies.

So here I am with my kitchen piled high with dirty dishes, my floor in need of mopping, my windows and glass doors spotted with food spills and small dirty handprints. But my husband just put dinner on the stove, my children are all in good spirits, and I am going outside. My daughters want to swing. They asked Mommy to push them. This time, the other things can wait.

THE TITLE OF THIS STORY IS BASED ON PSALM 127:5.

DeAnna Larson was born in Dallas, Texas. She is the fifth of seven children but the first to be born in the covenant. Her parents, John and Betty Anne Dean, were baptized and sealed before she was born. She has a bachelor's degree in elementary education from BYU-Provo and worked as a third grade teacher. She then became an academic advisor at BYU and later at Sam Houston State University in Texas. She has been a stay-at-home mom for the past nine years. She and her husband, Fred, have four children. With their move to Apple Valley in 2012, they created a music room on the first floor of their home. Playing the piano is one of DeAnna's favorite things, along with reading and cooking. She also has an affinity for the colors purple and hot pink.

Leaning on My Heavenly Father

BY DARIA GORDHAMER

MY NAME IS DARIA MARIE GORDHAMER. I became a member of The Church of Jesus Christ of Latter-day Saints when I was 20 years old. A day never goes by that I am not thankful for the missionaries who sought me out and taught me about Jesus Christ. The gospel has become an anchor in my life, keeping me at bay with the throws of life.

Right now I have five children, the oldest being 9 years old and down the line they go every two years. These four boys and one girl have blessed my life immensely. However, every day brings its ups and downs as a mother. There are tears to be wiped, hugs to be given, "sorry's" and "thank you's" to be said, manners to be taught, faces to be washed, dishes to washed and rewashed and rewashed, laundry to be cleaned (hopefully), arguments to be mended and made up, patience to be tried, trials to overcome, victories to be celebrated, and love to be compassionately given to children who are happy, sad, and completely frustrated. Everyday something can happen that can dampen my spirits, that is, if I let it.

Through this wonderful roller coaster of being a mom I have learned to lean on my Heavenly Father for help, to ask for patience when my patience seems to not be found, and to most importantly feel the tender mercies as I am forgiven of my many imperfections. I have tried very hard to laugh when in times I could easily cry. I have found it so much easier to remember the good in each one of my sweet spirits that I have been blessed with to nurture here on earth rather than dwell on the negative moments. I am pretty sure that I could have a funny or disastrous family story each day of my life. I will share one such day.

One Sunday morning I sent David with the three older kids to church as I waited for Andrew to wake up from his nap. As I entered sacrament meeting, this is what I saw: Elijah's church pants were too short (again!) and his white shirt was not all that white anymore. Eva's hair wasn't neatly brushed and done, and that poor girl only had pink church shoes to wear (that didn't match her yellow dress and that were three sizes too big for her), so she was shoeless and swinging her feet. Abram had worn a nice sweater to church, but it was so warm in the chapel he took it off. I then realized the blue T-shirt I had put on under his sweater had a picture of three goofy Vikings on it. Hmm, church appropriate? I think not. Andrew looked cute as ever (thank goodness one of my children was dressed nicely!), and baby Thomas was way too warm and was sporting paper rabbit ears Eva had made and taped onto his hat. I was obviously wearing the same outfit I always did since none of my clothes fit me after having a baby. I just had a "poor me" moment when I saw our family. I was thinking how much my family looked like a rag tag team. I thought in my mind that I had tried so hard to get the children to look nice and then they didn't look very "put together." I felt like it was all my fault.

Shortly after my "poor me" moment, I remembered that it was okay that we looked like this. What was more important is that we feel the Spirit (which I did) and that we try our best. I can always do a bit better in my life. Yes, it seems like I have a hard time getting out to shop and buy clothes that fit my ever-growing children, and my talent in dressing nicely wanes, but Christ lives! I can celebrate that knowledge and feel good about the plan of salvation, rather than be hung up on the little things that don't matter.

I testify that Heavenly Father and Jesus Christ live. I love them. I know that Joseph Smith restored the gospel in this dispensation. I know that the scriptures bear truth and that I can draw closer to our Savior as I read them. I know that I can live with my family again and forever as I heed the commandments and endure to the end. I know that Heavenly Father hears our prayers and answers each earnest plea. I know that we are all children of our Heavenly Father. In the name of Jesus Christ, amen.

Daria Gordhamer was born in Long Beach, California, and was baptized in Minneapolis in 1998. Her parents are Gary and Shirley Reboin. A stay-at-home mom, Daria has a B.A. in biology and chemistry from Augsburg College. She loves Tae kwon do, dancing, cooking, reading, and biking and playing with her five children. She and her husband, David, and the children moved to Apple Valley in 2000.

The Eternal Nature of Peanut Butter

BY SHANTEL GARDNER

WHEN I WAS THINKING about what I wanted to write, this experience came to me. I pushed it aside, but the impression kept coming back.

The Family Proclamation does not tell us what to *do*, it tells us *who we are* and *what our relationship is* to God and Jesus Christ. It also gives us incredible insight into the character of our Heavenly Parents. We are meant to learn how to be like our Savior in family units, and this is how it happens for me. God is good. So good.

Here is the story:

On this particular day my daughter Ella was having a bad day. She has Asperger's, a high-functioning form of autism. Most people in her world are not even aware that she has this. I don't notice it most days, but this day I did. On her bad days she gets stuck in a rut, with a need for structure and for things to be and look a certain way. These days normally end up with her alone in her room, organizing her toys until she feels better. My mood on this day was of no help to her. She had come home from school

This is my daughter Ella. Isn't she just cute? And so big, making her own peanut butter and chocolate sandwich for lunch. (She calls Nutella chocolate. I guess she thinks she is getting away with something.) I took this picture to remember this experience.

and wanted to make her own lunch. I usually have her lunch premade, so it is waiting when she walks through the door, but I had a crazy morning, so this did not happen. When Ella is having a bad day, she will not compromise or rationalize. She is not able to have a two-sided discussion. She will even lose her language if it gets really bad. I have found the best thing to do is give her what she wants as reasonably as possible and try to curb bad behavior with distraction. Anyway, here was our dialogue:

Me: "Ella, do you want a peanut butter or circle sandwich for lunch?" *("Circle" is bologna. Long story.)*

Ella: "Peanut Butter Chocolate. I want to do it!" *(High-pitched scream)*

Me: "Okay, Ella. Let me help you."

Ella: "No! I do it!" *(Scream)*

Me: "Okay."

So I watched her proceed. She got a stool, climbed up to the counter. Couldn't reach the bread. She started screaming.

Me: "Ella, do you need help?"

Ella: "Bread!" *(Language now down to one word. This was not headed in a good direction.)*

So I got up to help her. I reached for the bread.

Ella: "NO!"

Me: "DO you want the bread?"

Ella: "Ella Do!" *(Scream)*

Me: "Okay."

She struggled a few seconds.

Ella: "Please help."

So I helped her get the bread out and laid out the slices for her. I magically and very sneakily managed to get out the jars she needed and unscrew the tops without her protesting. I handed her the butter knife.

She proceeded to dig into the peanut butter and the Nutella. She was making a huge mess. I was having a very hard time not intervening. Not only was she making a complete mess of everything, but she was getting upset. She was piling way too much on the bread, she was taking way too long, and I had a long list of other things I did not like about this situation. Finally, after about ten minutes, she was done with one piece. It was literally a mountain of peanut butter. She and the counter were covered. I was not happy. I was dwelling on how my day had been so far, how she was likely going to need a bath after this, and how a bath would lead into the afternoon, and then the kids would be home from school. I was getting overwhelmed quickly. She started screaming again. I started to cry; I felt done. The sound hurt my ears and my heart. I didn't know what to do. What did she want now?

Me *(through tears)*: "What, Ella?"

Ella: "Fix it!"

I didn't know what she meant, so I got up and looked at the disaster on the counter.

Ella *(very quietly and completely unlike the way she had been over the last thirty minutes)*: "Make it smoooooth."

She handed me the knife.

My despair at the situation was immediately transformed to deep peace and understanding at what I was being taught. As I followed Ella's instructions to smooth out the peanut butter perfectly and make it go "all the way to the edges" of the bread, I realized that we makes messes sometimes. We take situations in life and insist (sometimes screaming) on doing it all ourselves. We make mistakes, we misjudge, mistrust, and misuse sometimes. We cause a lot of grief to the people around us as we learn, and we judge others harshly as they learn. Then we give our slice of peanut butter bread to the Savior, and He makes it all smooth. He makes it perfect. He spreads it to the edges of the bread and makes our work look like it was done by a professional chef. Then he lets us keep it. To savor and find joy in. As we become confident in the Savior's ability to perfect our efforts, we become stronger and our capacities increase.

I grabbed the camera and took a picture and really enjoyed letting Ella make the rest of the sandwich. I enjoyed the process of watching her learn, and I was ready to step in when she needed me. Happily and patiently this time, I felt so grateful to my Heavenly Father for taking what was a mess and making it a moment of learning never to be forgotten.

Shantel Gardner was born in Roosevelt, Utah, to Clyde and Shirley Bancroft. She lives in Minnesota with her husband, Joel, and their five children. She is a student in the honors program at the University of Minnesota, majoring in US History and Religious Studies with a minor in Jewish Studies. She is also a research historian for the University and the Minnesota Historical Society. She serves on the board of the Joseph Smith Jr. and Emma Hale Smith Historical Society and travels to universities and historical sites to speak about the lives and legacies of Joseph and Emma. Being a descendent of the Joseph Smith family line is a treasure, and its discovery a tender mercy from the Lord. Her favorite place is Winter Quarters. Shantel also considers chocolate necessary to her salvation and partakes as often as she can.

*And how merciful is our God unto us, for he remembereth
the house of Israel, both roots and branches; and he stretches forth
his hands unto them all the day long.
Jacob 6:4*

Testifying of
Gospel Truths

My Baptism Day

BY EMMA THATCHER

WHEN IT WAS TIME FOR ME TO GET BAPTIZED, we had to make a decision. We had moved to Minnesota the year before, but most of my family and friends were still in Utah. I wanted to get baptized in my old ward in Salt Lake City. My parents said yes and so we made plans for me to get baptized on my mom's birthday, May 9, at the LeGrand ward building in Salt Lake City.

On the day of my baptism we went to the Garden Park ward building in the morning to take pictures. That chapel is just two blocks away from where I would be getting baptized, but it has a pond with a bridge and a pretty garden. My mom's friend took photos of me and my brother, Caleb. I love to look at those photos now to remember how special my baptism day was.

After the photos, we went out to lunch near my old house. It made me sad that we had moved to Minnesota, but I was also happy that I could be with my friends and family for my baptism.

The pictures from the day of my baptism remind me how I felt the Spirit when I was baptized and confirmed.

My old Primary teachers gave the talks, and my dad baptized me. I still remember how I felt when I went under the water. I really did feel clean and pure and happy. I knew that what I was feeling was the Holy Ghost. I knew that the decision I was making was right and that Heavenly Father loved me.

Then I was confirmed and received the gift of the Holy Ghost. I really felt the Spirit again and felt happy that I could have that feeling with me all the time as I chose the right. Getting baptized helped strengthen my testimony.

It has been four years now since the day I got baptized. I have been to many baptisms since then, of my friends, other kids in Primary, and people that the missionaries have taught. Because the elders used to live in our basement and now my dad is the ward mission leader, our family has helped the missionaries a lot. I really like going to baptisms because it reminds me of my own baptism. And at every baptism I attend I feel the Spirit. I know that Spirit is telling everyone there that the Church is true. I am grateful to be a member of this Church and I know it's true.

Emma Thatcher was born in Walnut Creek, California, lived for a time in Utah, and in 2008 moved to Minnesota. Her parents are Daniel and Holly (Nelson) Thatcher. Emma is going into seventh grade at Scott Highlands Middle School in Apple Valley. Her favorite subject in school is American Studies. She is also interested in fashion. She likes reading, doing hair, exercising at the YMCA, and hanging out with friends.

Come unto the Knowledge of the Truth

BY SANDRA MARIE CLUFF

I CELEBRATED MY 21ST BIRTHDAY in the Missionary Training Center in Provo, Utah. I had been called to serve in the Indiana Indianapolis Mission, and I loved everything about the MTC. I loved my companion, the elders in our district, and the knowledge of our instructors. There is something that can't compare to hundreds of missionaries and the Spirit meeting together for the single purpose of building up the kingdom of God.

My first mission area was a very small town in Indiana named Linton. My companion was a year older than I, and I was very excited to get to work. We tracted many of the first weeks I was on my mission searching for those who had been prepared to hear the truthfulness of the gospel on the earth today. We walked rural roads of even smaller towns where dirt roads did not have names to identify them. It was on one of these dusty dirt roads that I would use a golf ball to knock on the door of a trailer. (Golf balls resounded well on doors and saved our knuckles during the long days of tracting.)

Sandra Cluff: "Come unto a Knowledge of the Truth" 295

A tall man appearing to be in his late 60s answered the door, and I introduced us as sister missionaries from The Church of Jesus Christ of Latter-day Saints. I explained that we had a message we would love to share with him. He smiled, then nodded and invited us in. I scanned the room briefly, and it was clear that this man had traveled the world and loved books. He introduced himself as Larry Zinn and told us that he was a professor at the university. Being that I hadn't been in the mission field for very long, I was a bit nervous when I heard the word professor and even more nervous when I found he studied philosophy and Eastern religions. I kept my composure and entertained his questions. He seemed inquisitive at first at why two young women would be tracting door-to-door, talking about God. We gave a brief message about God's prophets throughout the ages in preparation to teach him about the First Vision on our next visit. He seemed engaged in the discussion and happily accepted a return appointment for the next week.

I studied more fervently throughout the next week preparing for any questions that may come into play in our next discussion. The people of Indiana love their Bibles and know them well. I was confident in my teaching abilities and knew the material of the discussions well, but I didn't want to be caught off guard. Well, to make a long story short, it would have never crossed my mind to study the test question I would be given by the professor.

My companion and I returned to Mr. Zinn's home to teach him about the Prophet Joseph Smith, the First Vision, and the Book of Mormon. At the end of the first discussion we were to invite him to be baptized as outlined in the discussion manual. I was teaching the lesson this day. Surprisingly I didn't feel nervous

Here I am as a brand new missionary. At that time sisters had to be 21 before entering the mission field. I was one of the youngest because I celebrated my 21 birthday in the MTC.

at all but was empowered by the Spirit as I taught the gospel to him. I could feel the presence of the Spirit strongly in the room as I spoke of the gospel truths. When I had finished the discussion and knew that the Spirit was there so strongly, I challenged Mr. Zinn to be baptized into the Church of Jesus Christ. I had never done this before, but everything was falling into place, or so I thought.

Mr. Zinn sat there for a moment and then went and got a large book out of his vast collection in his library. I noticed it was an astronomy book. I couldn't figure out what was going on at first. He opened the book to a double-paged picture of our solar system and asked me to point to where God lived. He said that if I could tell him where God lived in that picture, he would then join our church. I was a bit perplexed and taken aback. I knew God lives in the heavens in a place named Kolob, but I did not know a specific spot in the universe to identify to Mr. Zinn. Believe me when I tell you, that was not something they taught us in the Missionary Training Center.

I know it was only moments, but it seemed like an eternity in my mind. Then the Spirit brought to my mind the scripture in 2 Timothy, chapter 1, verses 7–8, which reads: "For God hath not given us the spirit of fear; but of power, and of love, and of a sound mind. Be not thou therefore ashamed of the testimony of our Lord."

The answer had come to me through the Spirit of the Holy Ghost to simply bear my testimony: I do not know where exactly in the map of the galaxy God lives, but I do know that God does live and that He loves all of His children. I know that He sent his Son Jesus Christ to be sacrificed for our sins so that we could repent and become perfected through His name. I know that Heavenly Father and Jesus Christ appeared to a young, uneducated farm boy named Joseph Smith. I know that Joseph Smith would be schooled in the ways of God and become the chosen prophet of this dispensation to restore in its entirety the gospel of Jesus Christ. I know he translated the Book of Mormon by the power of God. I know that the Book of Mormon testifies of Jesus Christ and that by reading and praying about its content, it will help us gain a testimony of God and the plan of happiness. I ended my testimony in the name of Jesus Christ.

I felt the whole room fill with the Spirit so strongly. The Holy Ghost was in the room fully to testify of the divinity of God the Father and His Son Jesus Christ. I was overcome with emotion and I felt mentally exhausted. I looked to Mr. Zinn and waited for a response. He appeared to be unphased by my testimony or the presence of the Holy Ghost. I was confused. How could I feel the presence of the Spirit so strongly and he feel nothing? I know that I was younger, less traveled, and certainly less educated than Mr. Zinn, but I also recognized that I possessed the most important knowledge that could be obtained. I had a testimony of the restored gospel of Jesus Christ. He thanked us for our time, and we left his home knowing that we would never return.

Paul describes the apostasy and perilous times of the last days in 2 Timothy, chapter 3, verses 2, 5, and 7: "For men shall be lovers of their own selves, covetous, boasters, proud, blasphemers... Having a form of godliness, but denying the power thereof... Ever learning, and never able to come to the knowledge of the truth."

Mr. Zinn had missed the mark entirely. He was unable to endure sound doctrine and turned away from the truth. His heart was indeed hard, and my testimony fell upon deaf ears. I learned a very important lesson that day, and I have reflected on it many times over the years. I am older now, I have educational degrees, I have traveled the world, but I recognize that without God I am nothing. I have witnessed those I love fall into the trap of intellectualism. I know that intellectualism is not the Lord's end goal and never will be. All of the learning and worldly accolades gain us nothing unless we come unto the knowledge of the truth.

Paul gives us counsel on how we should conduct our lives in 2 Timothy, chapter 3, verses 14-17:

> But continue thou in the things which thou hast learned and hast been assured of, knowing of whom thou hast learned them;
> And that from a child thou hast known the holy scriptures which are able to make thee wise unto salvation through faith which is in Christ Jesus.

> All scripture is given by inspiration of God, and is profitable for doctrine, for reproof, for correction, for instruction in righteousness;
>
> That the man of God may be perfect, thoroughly furnished unto all good works.

So I implore you, that the next time you are caught in a situation and are not sure how to proceed, just look to the heavens and proclaim, "My God, how great Thou art!

Sandra Marie Cluff was a Navy brat who never had to move. She was born and raised in National City, San Diego, California. Her parents are the late Arthur "O" and Penny Marie Burch. Sandra has a B.S.N. from Graceland College and was working as a nurse in Provo, Utah, when an answer to prayer directed her to move to Apple Valley where her brother and family had just settled. That was 1989. She did postgraduate work in nursing at the University of Minnesota. She later became Hennepin County Nurse of the Year and is a Certified Critical Care Nurse and a Certified Nephrology Nurse. She has also lobbied on behalf of nursing at the capital. Being single until age 36 gave her many opportunities for service in the Church. Among these were her mission to Indiana and a music mission touring as a vocalist with the Mormon Youth Symphony and Chorus. She and her husband, Kevin, adopted three beautiful children. Sandra has an endless list of interests, including politics, law, singing, piano, scrapbooking, emergency preparedness, musical theatre dinner parties, poetry, traveling, photography, and fishing, to name a few.

Learning about the Savior

BY SARAH PETERSON

ONCE WHEN I WAS 8 YEARS OLD, the Primary presidency put together a few different activities for us on the Saturday before Easter. As a group we walked from the first classroom to the second and learned about the Atonement and Christ's Resurrection. In one of the rooms we looked at items inside eggs, such as a red ribbon to signify the robe that the soldiers put on Jesus, and read the attached scriptures.

After visiting the two classrooms, we all convened in the Primary room to watch a video that talked about the last week of the Savior's life. As the video was wrapping up, a song that we had recently learned started playing. The video displayed pictures of Christ, such as when He was giving the Sermon on the Mount. First one child started singing softly and then everyone quietly joined in, even the leaders. It was such a peaceful and spirit-filled moment. I truly felt the love of God and Jesus Christ for me. It was one of the first times I ever remember feeling the Spirit that strongly.

Sarah Peterson was born in American Fork, Utah, and she was living in Ohio before moving to Apple Valley, Minnesota, with her family in August 2010. Her parents are Lance and Jessica Peterson, and she has three brothers and a sister. In the fall Sarah will enter eighth grade at Falcon Ridge Middle School where she participates in school plays and musicals. She loves to sing, read, and play the piano. She also plays violin in the orchestra. She is interested in studying music or marine biology in college.

And this is my glory, that perhaps I may be an instrument in the hands of God to bring some soul to repentance, and this is my joy.
Alma 29:9

We Are His Daughters

BY JANNICA VILLANUEVA

YOU ARE SONS AND DAUGHTERS of our Heavenly Father." That's a phrase that we've heard since we were little, especially as children growing up in the Church. It's been reiterated so many times that it sometimes loses its meaning to me.

I know that I am a daughter of God, but it's so easy to forget our divine potential and individual worth. It's easy to think badly of ourselves and of others especially during trying times in our lives. We need to realize that we are truly and wholeheartedly His children, that He loves us and cares for us and He knows our potential and what we're capable of. We can't comprehend His vast love for us, but He knows us. He knows the inner workings of our hearts, and He understands our problems and our trials. We are His children and He will always be there for us.

I know that the Church is true. I know that our Heavenly Father loves us and that Jesus Christ sacrificed His life to save us. I have faith in the love and mercy of our Heavenly Father and Jesus Christ, and I know that as long as we repent and follow the commandments, we will always find our way back into the light of Christ.

Jannica Villanueva is planning to study social sciences in college and eventually go on to medical school. Meanwhile, this fall she will attend East View High School as a senior. Jannica was born in Quezon City, Philippines, and moved to Apple Valley, Minnesota, with her family in 2007. Her parents are Elmer and Abegail Villanueva. Jannica volunteers with Youth Teaching Youth and Project Explorers. She loves to read and travel with her family and friends.

"O Death,
Where Is Thy Sting?"

BY KRYSTAL FLOHR

IN OUR FIRST FEW YEARS OF MARRIAGE, Tyson and I lived in my parents' basement apartment. My older sister Jennifer also lived at home. I loved the time spent with my family. We were all extremely close.

Then in August 2007 doctors found a mass in my father's bladder. I alone accompanied my parents to the hospital and waited the long hours outside surgery with my mother. I held her hand as the doctor explained how large the mass was, how difficult it was to remove, and how long the treatment that lay ahead of him would be. A grey and frail body replaced the once strong and chipper man that was my father. I joked lightheartedly with my parents to brighten their spirits, but in my own quiet moments I greatly feared a nearing presence of death. I could hardly bear the thought of losing my father.

After a week in recovery at the hospital, my father's strength was sufficient for him to return home. Jennifer left that very weekend to continue her education in southern Utah. Sunday evening

Tyson and I were enjoying a movie together when I saw my father, red-faced at our door. When he came in, he fell to the floor sobbing. Jennifer had been killed in a car accident. I remember feeling very ill and retreating to the bathroom.

Those first few days were a mess of people coming and going to offer their comfort and condolence, but they could bring no peace. Family came and went, flowers arrived and wilted. My own pain at the loss of my sister was greatly overshadowed by the immense grief of my parents. I tried desperately to fill the void that was left in their lives. But I alone could not pacify their pain.

In 1969 Elsabeth Kubler-Ross developed what she called the five stages of loss and grief. She said these are universal and are experienced by people from all different walks of life. I believe her.

1. *Denial and Isolation.* I thought, surely this was a mistake. They are wrong, it couldn't have been Jennifer.

2. *Anger.* I became very angry, with God a little, but more so with Jennifer. How could she leave our family? How could she go and hurt Mom and Dad so deeply?

3. *Bargaining.* Take me instead? Can't she just be injured or paralyzed? Can't we receive a different trial?

4. *Depression.* I became a recluse, quit my job, and isolated myself.

5. *Acceptance.* Many people suffering from grief never achieve this stage, but through faith in Christ, how can they not?

In April 1996 President Gordon B. Hinckley gave his "This Glorious Easter Morn" talk in which he presented a beautiful account of the Atonement and Resurrection. He said, "Those who hated Jesus thought they had put an end to Him forever when the cruel spikes pierced His quivering flesh and the cross was raised on Calvary. But this was the Son of God, with whose power they did not reckon. Through His death came the Resurrection and the assurance of eternal life."

President Hinckley called the Resurrection "the greatest victory of all time, the victory over death." He taught, "There is nothing more universal than death, and nothing brighter with hope and faith than the assurance of immortality. The abject sorrow that comes with death, the bereavement that follows the passing of a loved one are mitigated only by the certainty of the Resurrection of the Son of God that first Easter morning."

As members of The Church of Jesus Christ of Latter-day Saints, we are not immune to the grief and pain of losing a loved one, but we, perhaps above all others, can experience that brightness of hope that can only come from our testimony of the Risen, Living Savor. Because He led the way to immortality, we too will rise. We will be reunited with our loved ones and spend the eternities together. That was the comfort and reassurance my parents needed. It was what I needed to strengthen my testimony in my Savior, Jesus Christ, and know that He lives.

We were very new in the ward, and so I was a bit shocked recently when Brother Rob Amott, without knowing me, asked me to give a sacrament meeting talk on topic of death and resurrection. He could not have known that this subject would hit so close to home and at such a tender time. My talk was given in the same week that our family celebrated Jennifer's birthday, followed by the birthdays of my husband and my father.

There were many months that I wasn't sure that my loving father would be able to bear such a great loss. I know that there were times when he wished to give up in his battle of cancer and join my sister in the spirit world. However, despite the overwhelming physical challenges at the time of the loss of his daughter, he has been made whole once again and is strengthened by his love and testimony of Christ.

Heavenly Father knows what pains we are able to bear and the trials that will strengthen us. Because of the experiences of that summer and the healing process in the years that followed, I have gained an unwavering testimony in the Atonement and Resurrection of our beloved brother, Jesus Christ. I have a great testimony of eternal families and the sacred ordinances performed in holy temples. In the years following his talk, President Hinckley suffered the loss of his beloved eternal companion, as President Monson does now. However, these great men above all others know of the surety, as do I, that He is risen. In the name of Jesus Christ, amen.

The title of this story is quoted from 1 Corinthians 15:55.

Krystal Flohr was born in Salt Lake City, Utah, but grew up in Tillamook, Oregon, the "Land of the World's Best Cheddar Cheese." Both of her parents, Morris and Cindy Grover descend from Mormon pioneers. Her husband, Tyson, was a convert to the Church in 2004. She met him in Illinois when they were working at the same gym. She eventually told him that if he moved to Oregon she would marry him, and he accepted. Krystal studied art at BYU and is currently a stay-at-home mom with two little boys. She paints watercolors, does portrait photography, and do-it-yourself projects. She likes to work out and loves food. She is also a writer.

These Things
I Know

BY LISA FLAKE

I HAVE RECOGNIZED THE HAND OF THE LORD many times in my life, daily in fact. While I have witnessed miracles occasionally, I recognize the Lord in the small and simple things of my life: the whisperings of the Spirit in answer to prayer, the uplifting words of a friend, the hug of a child, the beauty of God's creations. All remind me that the Lord is a part of my life.

Right now I am entering a new stage in my life. My children are beginning to leave home. This gives me cause to reflect upon my job as mother. I ask myself, "How have I done? Are testimonies rooted deep within my children? Could they say, as the stripling warriors said in Alma 56:48, 'We do not doubt our mothers knew it'?"

So, at this time, I just want to leave my testimony of *what I know*. I know that God lives and deeply loves each of His children. I know He hears and answers the sincere prayers of His children. I know Jesus Christ showed us the way to live that will bring peace in this life and happiness in the next. He is our Savior and Redeemer, our Advocate and our Friend. I love Them both and am so grateful for what They do for me each day. I believe the Book of Mormon was inspired of God and written by prophets and that it was brought forth by inspiration through the prophet, Joseph Smith. I believe Joseph Smith saw God the Father and Jesus Christ and that Christ's church and gospel were restored to the earth through Joseph Smith. I believe we are guided today by a living prophet and, if we follow his guidance, given to him by Heavenly Father, we can find joy and peace today and forever. I am thankful for the restoration of the priesthood and for all that means in my life. It means I can repent, partake of the sacrament, and be renewed. It means I can be healed and strengthened through blessings. It means all things I hold dear to me can be forever—most important of which are my family relationships because of temple covenants.

My hope and prayer are that my children and all who are in my sphere of influence know that this is my testimony and that I *know it.* I hope that I and they together can have the same said of us that was said of the stripling warriors in Alma 53:20-21, "and they were exceedingly valiant for courage, and also for strength and activity; but behold, this was not all—they were men [and women] who were true at all times in whatsoever thing they were entrusted. Yea, they were men of truth and soberness, for they had been taught to keep the commandments of God and to walk uprightly before him."

Lisa Flake moved with her family to Minnesota in 2012. She was born in Omaha, Nebraska, the daughter of Neil and LaNae Morgan, and is of rich Mormon pioneer descent. She graduated from Utah State Universidty with a B.S. in business information systems and is currently a stay-at-home mom. She and her husband, Maury, have four children.

Behold the wounds which pierced my side, and also the prints of the nails in my hands and feet; be faithful, keep my commandments, and ye shall inherit the kingdom of heaven Amen.
Doctrine & Covenants 6:37

Index

The information contained in the authors' biographies is not indexed.

Amott, Ande, 263-267

Anderson, Dianne, 24-28

Animals, 74,181-183, 203-204. *See also Snake.*

Answers to Prayer. *See Prayer, Promptings.*

Atonement, 4, 12, 81, 205, 237-238, 278, 300, 305-307

Automobile accidents, 85-86,154, 241-245, 303-307

Bailey, Nikhom, 115-116

Balcha, Haymanot, 187-188

Baptism, 10,12, 15, 23, 25, 29-30, 45, 47-48, 291-293; for the dead, 197, 213-215

Barringer, Mindy, 99-100

Beauty of nature, 203-204, 209-210, 224-226

Bible, 15, 19, 27, 41, 43, 45, 255-256, 295

Blessing, priesthood, 23, 119, 122, 165-166, 175, 182, 266, 309

Blessings, gratitude for, 1, 4, 30-31, 195; blessings, recognized, 12, 22, 83, 95-96, 131, 163, 183,

276; blessings for righteous living, 161, 184

Book of Mormon, 8-9, 18-19, 27, 43, 45, 197, 228, 252-253, 295-297. 309; Lehi's dream, 264-266

Calistro, Barbara, 246-247

Calling, 26, 82-84, 108-109, 257

Cancer. *See Health Issues.*

Car accidents. *See Automobile accidents.*

Career. *See Employment.*

Children, in family, 7-10, 23, 25, 37-38, 4-43, 141, 181, 192-195, 196, 248, 250, 255-256; learning from children, 55-57, 85-86, 215-217; God's children, 201, 214, 297, 302. *See Mothering, Pregnancy.*

Clifford, Tamara, 117-120

Cluff, Sandra Marie, 294-299

Conversion, 7-10, 11-13, 14-16, 17-23, 24-25, 29-31, 32-36, 37, 41-46, 47-48, 115, 161, 187, 203, 221-222, 231, 246, 252-253, 256-257, 294

Daughter of God, 26, 98, 106, 205-206, 209-210, 211, 214, 302-303

Davis, Ainsley, 66

Davis, Frances, 32-36, 273-274

Davis, Loni, 90-92, 241-245

Death, 43-44, 117, 145-147, 227-230, 241-245, 246-248, 304-308; in memoriam, 241-245, 246-248, 255-259

Depression, 7, 29, 63, 95-96, 112, 203, 209-210, 211, 305

Douangphouxay, Chay, 249-254

Drawing closer to God. 201-202, 203-204, 205-206, 207-208, 209-210, 211, 213-214, 215-218. *See Love of God and Christ for us.*

Dreams (prophetic), 43, 87, 193-195; Lehi's dream, 264

Dufur, Dannica, 181-183

Education, 11, 87-89, 130-131, 169, 252-253, 296-298

Ekanem, Lucy, 11-13, 79-81

Employment, 14, 38, 88-89, 96, 99, 102, 115-116, 121-124, 131, 169, 184, 192-194, 201, 221, 305

Example, 163-164, 221-222, 227-229, 231-232, 233-328, 239-240, 246-248, 249-250, 255-260, 273-274

Faith, 110, 127-129, 130-132, 133-134, 135-136, 137-138. *See Answers to prayer, Conversion,* *Guidance on path of life, Tender mercies, Testimony.*

Family History, 150, 213-214, 244-245

Family. *See Father, Mother, Motherhood, Children, Grandparents.*

Father (earthly), 33-34, 48, 56, 74-75, 85-86, 99-100, 105, 113, 119, 122-123, 155, 161, 171, 205, 229, 236-237, 241, 249-250, 292, 304-307

Flake, Ashley, 137-138

Flake, Lisa, 308-309

Flohr, Krystal, 303-307

Friedman, Jessica, 209-210

Gandarilla, Maria, 161-162

Gardner, Brooklyn, 221-222

Gardner, Shantel, 283-287

Gayder, Nancy, 3, 14-16, 174-176

Gintz, Tonia, 17-23, 82-83

Glaser, Sonia, 127-129

God's love. *See Love of God and Christ for us, Daughter of God, Testimony.*

God's plan for individuals. *See Guidance on path of life.*

Gordhamer, Cara Marie, 168

Gordhamer, Daria Marie, 280-282

Gordhamer, Marlene, 189-191

Graham, Heather J., 4, 59-62

Graham, Kourtney Marie, 141-144

Index

Grandparents, 141-144, 221-222, 227-230, 233-238, 241-245, 249-253, 255, 274

Guidance on path of life, 11, 30, 95-98, 99-100, 101-106, 107-111, 112-114, 115-116, 117-120, 121-124, 130-13. *See Conversion, Promptings.*

Gunyan, Megan, 268-272

Hamer, Ginger, 82-84, 107-111

Health issues, 99, 145-147, 171-172, 174-176, 177-180, 205, 223-226, 227-230. *See Death, Pregnancy.*

Herrmann, Sabrina, 169-170

Hoffman, Hannah, 255-259

Hogge, Erika, 121-124

Holy Ghost, 1, 19, 26, 27, 48, 66, 146, 153-154, 213, 237, 271, 292, 297. *See Spirit.*

Hosman, Noël, 207-208

Housework, 90-93, 189-191, 278-279

Howze, Lynnette, 95-98

Husband, meeting him, 21, 39-40, 42, 60, 103-106, 119-120, 256, 275

Illness. *See Health Issues.*

Inspiration. *See Prayer, answers to; Promptings.*

Jensen, Cheryl "Cher", 203-204

Jesus Christ. *See Atonement, Testimony.*

Johnson, Diane, 37-40

Kellington, Jackie, 1, 3, 8, 41-46, 51-54, 85-86, 148-151, 192-195, 248, 255-260

Korth, Caroline, 145-147

Larson, DeAnna, 101-106, 275-279

Leavitt, Heather, 213-214

Love of God and Christ for us, 12, 23, 31, 32, 42, 72, 98, 106, 113, 117, 118, 119, 120, 122, 124, 127, 131, 136, 138, 140, 159-60, 166, 169, 189, 190, 198, 204, 206, 208, 209-210, 214, 216, 237, 238, 240, 253, 266, 282, 292, 297, 300, 302-303, 308; love for family and fellowmen, 83, 109-110, 112, 185, 194, 227, 229, 239, 245, 255, 271; feeling love, 15, 19, 26, 63. *See Daughters of God, Testimony.*

Maller, Trina, 231-232

Manar, Helen, 201-202

McAllister, Josalyn, 184-186

McGregor, Vicki, 171-173

Meyer, Amy, 130-132

Miller, Kristine, 223-226

Miracles, 25, 45, 72, 85-86, 127-128, 144, 149, 174-176, 177-180, 187, 252, 308

Missionaries, 8-9, 14-15, 17, 22, 24-25, 28, 29, 33-35, 37, 43-45, 112-113, 161, 221, 231, 252, 256, 280, 292; member missionaries, serving a mission, 8, 11, 34, 38-39, 47-48, 101, 148-150, 172,

187, 196-198, 207-208, 247, 275, 294-299

Mother, 29, 33, 42-43, 66, 74-77, 165, 194, 213, 223-226, 228, 232 244, 246, 250-253, 255-259, 304

Motherhood, 88-89, 131,154-155, 184-185, 210, 215-216, 263-267, 268-272, 273-274, 275-279, 280-282, 283-287, 308-309. *See Single mom.*

Move (relocate residence), 33, 37-39, 67-73, 79-81, 99-100, 101-102, 106, 112-113, 115-116, 121, 141, 184-185, 248, 291

Music, 104, 118, 152-156, 234, 237

Nielsen, Melissa, 4, 215-218, 233-238

Obedience, 127-128, 130-131, 133, 135-136, 137-138

Parsons, Polly J., 112-114
Peterson, Jessica Ann, 165-167
Peterson, Sarah, 300-301
Plan of salvation, plan of happiness, 27, 30, 44, 147, 150, 156, 230, 282, 297
Pratt, Merle, 70-71, 152-156
Prayer, 21, 27, 35, 41, 59-62, 95-96, 117, 155, 172, 182, 226, 252, 267, 271, 278, 282, 297, 308; answers to prayer, 8, 15, 19, 28, 44, 51-54, 55-58, 63-65, 66, 67-73, 74-78, 79-81, 82-84, 85-86, 87-89, 90-92, 102, 104-105, 107-109, 116, 118-119, 121-123, 127-128, 133,

135-136, 142-144, 166, 172, 178-179, 181-182, 203-204, 244, 256, 259, 275-276

Pregnancy, 112-113, 121-122, 130-131, 159-160, 177-180, 187, 227-228, 275-276

Priesthood, 39, 42, 101, 174-175, 280, 291

Prompting, 38, 40, 112-113, 141-143, 145-147, 148-151, 152-156, 160, 177-179, 185, 236-238, 297, 306. *See Holy Ghost; Prayer, answers to; Spirit.*

Prophet. *See Testimony*
Pugmire, Allie Darlene, 163-164
Pugmire, Anna, 133-134
Pugmire, EmRee M., 196-198

Restoration, 31, 42-43, 117, 148, 172, 256, 287, 297-298, 309
Robinson, Caitlin, 29-31

Savior. *See Jesus Christ.*
Schweigert, Krissy, 177-180
Scripture reading, 8-9, 18-19, 27, 63, 96, 109-110, 155, 163, 282, 297
Service, 61, 83, 109, 135-136, 155; exemplified in lives, 246-248, 255-260
Singer, Cindy, 159-160
Single mom, 17, 161, 169, 187, 250
Snake, 74-77, 166-167
Spirit (of the Lord), 3, 23, 30, 37, 38, 40, 59-61, 63, 71, 86, 103, 113, 117-118, 123, 128, 141, 148-150, 154-156, 185, 228, 245, 252, 264,

267, 270-271, 277-278, 282, 292-293, 300, 308. *See Holy Ghost; Prayer, answers to; Prompting.*

Storland, Norma, 47-48, 246-248

Stotts, Maria, 239-240

Stotts, Marissa, 211-212

Stotts, Megan, 63-65

Temple, 10, 22, 25, 33, 35-36, 39-40, 48, 80, 96, 106, 150, 155, 168, 196-198, 207-208, 213-214, 229, 239-41, 244-245, 275, 307, 309; Oakland Temple pageant, 117-118, 236; temple open house, 11, 196

Tender Mercies, 130-131, 159-160, 161-162, 163-164, 165-167, 169-170, 171-173, 174-176, 177-180, 181-183, 184-186, 187-188, 189-191, 192-195, 196-198. *See Blessings; Miracles; Prayer, answers to.*

Tennant, Cathy, 87-89

Tennant, Emily, 74-78

Testimony, 4, 10, 11-12, 15, 45, 64, 66, 81, 95-98, 100, 110, 113, 116, 118, 119-120, 124, 128, 131, 136, 138, 147, 150, 160, 165, 166-167, 168, 169-170, 172, 180, 185-186, 189, 198, 205-206, 210, 213-214, 237-238, 253, 263, 267, 282, 292-293, 297-299, 302-303, 307, 308-309

Thatcher, Emma, 291-293

Thatcher, Holly, 4, 67-73

The Church of Jesus Christ of Latter-day Saints, the true Church, 14-15, 27, 293, 302

Tithing, 127-129

Villanueva, Abby, 55-58

Villanueva, Jannica, 302-303

Villanueva, Shekinah, 205-206

Visiting teachers, 170, 185, 231

White, Becky, 135-136

Word of Wisdom, 9, 14, 32, 38-39, 44-45

Young, Lisa, 4, **7**-10

Made in the USA
Lexington, KY
27 July 2018